The V

Dear

Thought This
might be
helpful ?
Much Love, as
always,

Jay

x

The Vicar's FAQ

All you ever wanted to know about
Christianity and the Church

Caroline Symcox

DARTON · LONGMAN + TODD

First published in 2013 by
Darton, Longman and Todd Ltd
1 Spencer Court
140 – 142 Wandsworth High Street
London SW18 4JJ

ISBN: 978-0-232-53022-3

A catalogue record for this book is available from the British Library

Phototypeset by Kerrypress Ltd, Luton, Bedfordshire
Printed and bound in Great Britain by Bell & Bain, Glasgow

Contents

Introduction: Being a Vicar

Welcome to *The Vicar's FAQ*! This book aims to answer all the questions you might ever have wanted to ask a vicar but never dared to ask/couldn't be bothered to corner them to ask/ thought you'd never get a straight answer to.

Before we get started, I want to make sure we're not working under false assumptions.

First, when I say 'vicar' I mean a Church of England vicar. What a vicar actually is and does we'll get to later, but right now I want us to be clear that I'm talking in terms of the Church of England, not Christianity in general, Roman Catholicism, the Russian Orthodox Church or any of the other numerous flavours of Christianity. That said, I will refer to other Churches where there are special distinctions or comparisons to the Church of England to be made.

Second, I don't speak for the whole Church of England. I don't think it's possible to come out with the absolute final word for such a wide variety of worshipping, believing people, and I'm not going to try. The answers I give to these frequently asked questions will be mine. Who I am and where I come from will obviously make a difference to what I think.

Finally, the questions and conversations that make up this book are a mixture of real questions that real people have come up and asked me, either in person or through the wonder of the internet, and questions that I've dreamed up, albeit based on real conversations. I won't be dodging the difficult ones – this isn't a propaganda effort.

So, shall we get started?

Who are you and why do you think you can answer my questions?

I'm Caroline. I'm a female, middle-class, southern English, thirty-something Christian, who also happens to be an ordained member of the Church of England.

A bit like the Vicar of Dibley?

Well, no. I don't have Dawn French's comic timing, but, more importantly, I'm not actually a vicar yet. I'm a curate, which is like an apprentice vicar. I have a vicar who's training me, and whom I follow around, learning how to do practical things like how to do a good wedding, or put together a funeral service. It's basically the final part of my training.

The hierarchy

Vicar, ordained, curate ... too many names. What's going on with all that?

Okay, the starting point in all this is 'ordained'. To be 'ordained' means to be selected and set apart for a particular purpose. It's related to the term 'ordered' – everything set in a particular place. When someone is ordained, they are selected by the Church and they go through a particular ceremony, where a bishop will lay his hands on the ordination candidate and pray that the Holy Spirit will empower them in the same way that it has empowered him. There are three layers in the Church to which people can be ordained. In order, they are deacon, priest and bishop. Everyone starts at the beginning and builds up the layers as the Church decides they are ready to move to the next level. So a bishop is already a priest and a deacon, for example.

What's the difference?

Each of these levels of ordination means you are authorised and empowered by the Church to do certain things. A deacon can lead worship and prayer, preach, take blessed bread and wine to the sick and housebound, and is especially encouraged to reach out in practical ways to the disempowered and helpless. A priest does all those things, but can also declare God's blessing and forgiveness and preside at services of Holy Communion – where people receive bread and wine as Christ's body and blood. A bishop in turn is able to do all those things but can also ordain others to be deacons and priests and confirm people at confirmation services.

Where do vicars come into it, then?

Well, although there are only three levels of ordination in the Church, there are lots of different jobs that people might do. The most important of these have particular titles attached to them. Everyone starts as a curate (or properly, an assistant curate), like me. We're apprentices, still learning.

But once you've finished your training, and once you've been ordained to the level of priest, there are lots of different jobs and roles open to you. You might become a vicar – that is, a priest with sole responsibility over a particular parish. But equally you might become a chaplain – working in a prison, a school, a university or a workplace. Or after a while you might be able to rise to positions of more responsibility, like an archdeacon, who has oversight of a number of vicars, or the dean of a cathedral who has charge of a whole cathedral and its people. To be any of these you have to be a priest first.

I thought vicars were Church of England and priests were Roman Catholic?

Nope. True, you'll generally only find Church of England priests referring to themselves as vicars or rectors, but the terms existed even before the Church of England broke away from the Roman Catholic Church. And your local vicar will certainly be a priest even if he or she doesn't use the term regularly.

What about 'ministers' or 'pastors' or 'clergy' or all those other words? Are they vicars too?

Sometimes. I'm not trying to be difficult! Within the Church of England you could use all of those for a vicar and it'd be right. In fact, you could use all of those for anyone ordained to any level, deacon, priest or bishop. But in different Christian denominations (a denomination is one of the subsets of Christianity, like Roman Catholic, Methodist, Baptist, Greek Orthodox and so on) the church leaders will often prefer one of those terms. Methodists like to call their congregation leaders 'ministers', for example.

   In my case I am all of the following: priest, curate, pastor, minister, ordained member of the Church, and member of the clergy. You could describe me and my role with any of those things. The opposite term is 'lay person'.

'Lay person'?

The term refers to those who are not ordained. It's usually used for congregation members, but can also be used more widely to include non-Christians.

I've heard of 'lay readers'. Does that mean they're not ordained? What do they do?

Lay readers, officially called 'Licensed Lay Ministers', are non-ordained people who are nevertheless called to serve in the Church. To become a lay reader requires passing a selection conference (much like a selection conference for those seeking to be ordained, which is explained below), and undergoing a period of training. Once they've passed the training they are licensed by the diocesan bishop, which makes it possible for them to lead certain worship services, preach, conduct pastoral care, and distribute the bread and wine at services of Holy Communion.

   You can tell who is a lay reader during a church service by what they wear. When clergy wear a cassock and surplice

they wear a black preaching scarf to complete the ensemble.
Lay readers on the other hand wear blue preaching scarves.
More on what all those things are in a second.

'Holy Communion'?

It's a service that includes the taking, blessing, breaking and
sharing of bread and the taking, blessing and sharing of wine. It
can also refer to the consecrated bread and wine themselves.
I'll go into what the whole service looks like, why we do it and
what it means in the chapters on worship and belief.

What are the different strata of the Church – what are the layers between vicars and archbishops?

This will probably make most sense as a diagram.

Curate

This is me!

|

(Associate priest)

An associate priest is someone who is ordained a priest and
has finished their training but hasn't yet been given sole
responsibility over a whole parish. They are part of a team of
other priests looking after what is usually a particularly large
parish, perhaps with lots of churches.

|

Vicar/rector

These are priests with sole responsibility over a parish. In a
parish, even if there are associate priests in the team, the buck
stops with the vicar or rector.

|

Area/rural dean

Priests who also oversee a collection of parishes. They are the go-to people if the vicar of one of those parishes has a problem. This collection of parishes is called a deanery.

|

Archdeacon

Priests who oversee a collection of deaneries, their vicars and deans, called (you guessed it) an archdeaconry.

|

Suffragan/area bishop

A full bishop, able to do all the things bishops do, but with responsibility over usually just a single archdeaconry, and under the authority of a diocesan bishop.

|

Diocesan bishop

A bishop with authority over a collection of Archdeaconries and their various people, called a diocese. Usually this will include two or three suffragan/area bishops and archdeacons and a large number of deaneries and parishes. There are over 40 diocesan bishops in the Church of England.

|

Archbishop

There are just two of these, the Archbishop of York, with responsibility for all the dioceses north of the Trent as well as the Isle of Man, which together are called the Province of York; and the Archbishop of Canterbury, who has responsibility for all the dioceses south of the Trent, together called the Province of Canterbury, along with authority over the entire Church of England.

|

The Queen

And lest we forget, the (non-ordained) figure at the head of this whole structure is the reigning monarch, who from the time of Henry VIII has been the supreme head of the Church of England.

There are two roles that priests might take that don't fit into this diagram. The first of these are chaplains, who work in a wide variety of different circumstances (prisons, schools, universities, factories, ships, the armed forces …), either individually or as members of a larger team. They are usually priests, but are employed by their workplace rather than by the Church itself. The second role is that of cathedral clergy. Priests who work in a cathedral are titled canons. They will generally be members of the cathedral 'chapter', the small council who run cathedral affairs, and their role in that council will form part of their title. So you will have the Canon Treasurer who looks after the cathedral's finances, or the Canon Precentor, who looks after the music and worship of the cathedral. The head of the whole cathedral is the Dean. This person is essentially the vicar of the cathedral – the buck stops with him or her.

Do you feel the Queen has much influence on doctrine?

It's really hard to say. The Queen is a devout Christian, and I'm sure when she meets with her chaplain and with the various bishops and archbishops she wouldn't hide how she felt about matters of doctrine. But at the same time the Church of England is a broad church. It holds plenty of differences of opinion under its roof, making it difficult to make pronouncements about what each and every one of us should believe. When pronouncements are made, they tend to be the end result of many years of work from specially formed groups, such as the Doctrine Commission.

So the straight answer would be: probably not, and certainly not directly.

Why chaplains in non-church places? What are they for?

Lots of people don't go to church. Lots of people don't go to church not because they don't believe in God or couldn't use the spiritual support, but because church services aren't at times or in places where they can usefully attend. That's what chaplains are for. Chaplains go into places and situations to reach people where they are, and give them the support they need. So they'll be in prisons, in hospitals, on mental health wards, at universities, and in the armed forces, to name just a few.

Just like vicars, they lead worship services, they pray, they spend time with people who need them to give counselling or support or spiritual guidance. The only difference is that they do it in circumstances other than your average parish church.

What's the difference between a vicar and a rector?

These days there isn't a real difference, although often the title of rector will come with a little more authority, especially in the context of a team parish, where several ordained ministers work as a team to serve a parish with a large number of different churches. Historically, the name vicar was given to a clergyman who was employed to take services in a church, while the rector was the person who had final authority for that church. That is to say, the rector, who was often the abbot of a local monastery, would hire a vicar to take services for him.

Roughly how big is a diocese, and what is the vicar responsible for there?

Dioceses vary hugely in size (in both geographical and population terms), thanks to differing population densities and where diocesan boundaries fell historically. After all, there have been dioceses since Saxon times. There are some geographically huge dioceses, largely made up of a lot of sparsely populated countryside, like Lincoln, Devon or Carlisle.

Then you get some much smaller ones which still have a lot of people in them, such as the dioceses around London: London, Guildford, Southwark and Rochester.

A vicar is always responsible for his or her parish within the diocese.

And a parish is?

A parish is a given area, whose boundaries can be drawn on a map. The whole of England is divided up into parishes. A parish can have just one church, but these days will usually consist of two or three, or many more, churches and congregations to be looked after. A vicar's parish is then grouped with others, first into a deanery, then the deaneries into an archdeaconry, and finally the archdeaconries into a diocese. Being part of the diocese means the vicar is answerable to the diocesan bishop in terms of planning, targets and so on.

Hold on, you've been talking about 'Church' with a capital C, and now you're talking about 'churches' with little cs. What's going on?

The Church with a capital C is the whole organisation. So when someone says 'I serve in the Church', you know they're not talking about the church down the road, but all Christian believers. In this book I'll be using it mainly to refer to the Church of England in particular. The term is often used to refer specifically to people, since it isn't the buildings that make people Christians.

A church with a little c is a building in which worship takes place.

The calling

Why? Become a vicar, that is?

If you ask a collection of people training to become vicars, chances are most of them would say they never really *wanted* to become vicars, they just felt very strongly that they *should*.

That's what vocation is, really. It's a strong sense that you are being called to be this particular kind of person and do these particular things to serve God and other people.

There are lots of wonderful things about being a vicar. There are also lots of less wonderful things. I'll go into those a bit more later. But really the heart of it is that you become a vicar because that's what you think God wants you to do.

What does that look like? How do you know what God wants?

It looks different to different people, so I can only really talk about my experience of being called. For me, first of all, it was a surprise. My family aren't particularly religious, and although I had chosen to go to church, that I would decide to become a vicar was by no means on the cards. When I was 16 years old or so, and praying one night, suddenly the thought that I should become a vicar came into my mind. I had always planned on becoming a vet, and I dismissed this strange stray thought about being ordained immediately. But it persisted. For years there was this sense of gentle pressure about what I should be doing in my life. I went through phases of wanting to follow where this sense of being pulled was leading, but then phases of pulling away and wanting to do anything but. On the way there was much soul searching, much prayer, much discussion and reading and thought. But finally I surrendered, and here I am.

How do you know what God wants? I believe it's about consistency and love. If that pull in a certain direction comes from a place of love and will result in more love in the world, and if that pull is consistent with what I know about God from my study and prayer, then I will trust that it is something that does indeed come from God.

Why a vicar particularly? Why not just be part of a congregation somewhere?

The simple answer is because I feel I *should* be a vicar. But putting the question of vocation aside, clergy are selected to perform a certain role within the Church. They are not better than the congregations they lead, or more holy, or more educated. But they are chosen by God and the Church and trained in certain practices, ways of thought and ways of being. So we need to have a set of skills that allows us to lead worship, to preach sermons, to teach, to listen and generally to live and act in a way that brings people to a better understanding of God. I believe I am someone who has the raw skills and temperament to be this particular person and do these particular things. Thankfully the Church believed the same thing!

The training

So how do you actually get to become a vicar?

It's all very well me believing that I've got the raw skills to do the vicaring thing, and that becoming a vicar is what God wants me to do, but for that to actually happen, the Church has to agree with me. Getting that to happen is a process.

The first step is recognising that you have a calling, and speaking to your local vicar about that. Often they'll give you opportunities to explore that vocation. They might give you more responsibilities within your local church, like leading a study group, distributing the bread or wine at Holy Communion services, leading elements of worship like public prayer or similar. There is also usually a vocation group in the area, which you might attend to hear more about becoming ordained and which allows you to make an informed decision about what God might be asking you to do.

Your vicar will also put you in touch with the diocesan director of ordinands. An 'ordinand' is a proto-vicar, someone who is in the process of either discernment (the phase before the big interview weekend) or training itself. So the diocesan director of ordinands, or DDO as they are more usually known, is the person whose job it is to assess and nurture potential vicars. It is their decision whether to put you forward for the three-day-long interview process that determines whether you can start the actual vicar training. The DDO will meet with you on a regular basis, ask you a lot of searching questions, get you to write essays, read books and fill out official paperwork. When they think you're ready, it's time for the big weekend of interviews and tests.

This final hurdle before training itself is the 'Bishop's Advisory Panel'. It's three days of being interviewed, producing a presentation, facilitating a discussion around that presentation, participating in others' discussions in a useful way, filling out psychological assessment paperwork and basically being watched like a hawk at all times, including mealtimes. How you get on with your fellow ordinands is just as important as what you say in your interviews. Needless to say it's stressful and exhausting and perhaps the hardest part of the whole process.

What does the Church look for in ordinands?

There are nine criteria that you are measured against during the assessment process. They are vocation, ministry within the Church of England, spirituality, personality and character, relationships, leadership and collaboration, faith, mission and evangelism, and, finally quality of mind.

What the Church is looking for is someone who believes they have a strong calling from God, who is flexible enough to work in the broad church that is the Church of England, who can work well with others, who has the potential to be a good leader, who is reasonably intelligent and questioning about their faith, who has a strong personal spirituality and relationship with God. Not much, eh? The assessors also look for integrity and the ability to handle pressure and stress with grace.

Does every potential vicar seriously have to measure up to all that? Wouldn't they have to be superhuman?

Yes and no. No one can get perfect scores on all those things, and most people will be much stronger in some areas and less so in others. The important thing is that the sum of the ordinand's parts measures up. Some elements of that list are musts, though. After all, certain things can be worked on through the training process, whereas others can't.

What would rule someone out?

First and foremost, if someone has any criminality in their past, the Church will look at them very carefully. Part of the documentation every ordinand has to produce is a CRB (Criminal Records Bureau) check, which will list all their past convictions. The findings of these checks are taken very seriously. Any convictions will warrant close investigation, and certainly if anything sexual or involving child abuse is found that candidate should go no further through the process.

There are also some positive qualities that an ordinand simply must have. If the ordinand doesn't seem to have a strong calling, for example, that's a deal-breaker. Similarly, if they're not spiritual people from the start, that's no good.

Those obvious things aside, though, it's pretty tough to get through the selection, and plenty of great people aren't selected to train simply because the selectors don't think they're the right combination of calling, temperament, qualities and skills to fit this particular role.

What does training to be a vicar involve?

Training falls into two parts. The first part is formal teaching, either as a residential student in a theological college or as a non-residential student learning through weekend seminars and similar.

'Theological college'?

These are places of learning like any other college, and are often attached to a nearby university. There are 22 training institutions that offer ordination training, 12 of which accept residential students.

Wait. What does 'theological' mean?

'Theology' comes from the Greek words for 'God' and 'words', or 'wisdom'. So it means the study of God and religion. Theology as a discipline can be practised with regard to and within many different religions. For example, 'Buddhist theology' or 'Hindu theology'. However, more usually in this country the word refers to 'Christian theology', the study of what Christian believe and why. Many different disciplines feed into theology as a whole subject area, including literary criticism of the Bible and other religious texts, historical study and philosophy. More recently, the other social sciences have also had a place in theological study, so there's plenty of input from psychology and sociology, for example.

The aim of theology is to answer questions ranging from: 'Does God exist?', 'What has Jesus got to do with God?' to 'What did the earliest Christians believe?' or 'Does prayer have an effect on people's mental health?'

Most theologians will specialise in a particular area. Vicars, of course, need to have a basic knowledge of everything.

So what do you do? Do non-residential students do the same stuff?

During this time you will need to gain some kind of theology degree, what kind depends on the qualifications you have already. If you have a theology degree already you will generally only train full time for two years and gain either a Masters degree, a Master of Theology (MTh) or Master of Arts (MA), or a postgraduate diploma. If you don't have a theology degree, you might go for a Bachelor of Arts degree or a foundation course in theology. Most ordinands will train full time for two years (part-time courses usually take longer), but those under 30 years of age or who are studying for the BA will usually take three years. In some rare cases, such as with an immensely experienced member of the Church or when an ordained minister of a different denomination such as a Baptist or Methodist minister wishes to become a Church of England priest, they can study for just one year.

As well as studying for a degree, ordinands practise and are assessed on a variety of practical skills that will be needed. These include things like preaching, singing and active listening. My theological college also ran 'themed study weeks' at the beginning and end of each term which taught more practical skills. I'm sure other colleges do similar things.

One thing that can't be taught but is mentioned a lot during training is so-called 'formation'. This is the process of questioning and maturing in your personal faith and sense of vocation which is inevitable and necessary through these intense years. Ordinands are supposed to emerge at the end of the training process as different people. The head of my theological college likened this to being 'in the belly of the whale' in the story of Jonah and the whale. There's a lot of being frustrated and unsure and insecure. Overcoming all that and finding a new stability is vitally important if you're to be a decent vicar in the fullness of time.

What do you mean by 'frustrated and unsure and insecure'?

Being an ordinand is extremely challenging. You are learning a lot about your religion and faith that might be surprising and unwelcome. For example, many ordinands find learning about the history of the Bible difficult because it challenges assumptions about what it means to call the Bible the 'word of God' (more on this in the section on belief). At the same time, you are living and learning with other ordinands, who often have different beliefs, practices and worship styles which may well challenge your own. Every ordinand will find themselves questioning whether they *really are* called by God at some point in the formation process.

And the second part of training?

Once you've finished your two- or three-year course, gained satisfactory marks and, most importantly, shown the necessary personal development, you'll be ordained deacon (the first level of ordination) and go on to the second stage of your training – your curacy.

What goes on in a curacy?

This is the period of being a curate, where I am now. It's the three- or four-year period of on-the-job learning that makes up the second part of training. The starting point is choosing *where* to do it. This is more complicated than it sounds.

Parishes that want to have a curate will put together a parish profile document, saying what they're about and what they're looking for in a curate. At the same time, you as an ordinand will fill out a form saying what you're looking for in a parish and will send along an updated CV.

Usually your home diocese, where you worshipped before you started training, will look at the profiles on the one hand and the ordinand documents on the other and will try to match up ordinands with parishes. However, sometimes a diocese won't have enough of its own ordinands to fill all the parish vacancies. If this happens, all the excess parish profiles will be sent out to theological colleges.

On the other hand, sometimes a diocese will have far too many ordinands for the number of parishes looking for new curates. In this case they will 'release' the ordinands they can't match to their own vacancies, and those ordinands will be set loose to find their own parish in which to be a curate. Which is where that pile of parish profiles sent to the colleges comes in. Ordinands will take profiles off the pile until they find one they think they might fit.

Who chooses whom?

It's a bit like internet dating. You both look at each other's profiles. If you like what you see, you organise a first date. In fixing up a curacy, this first date is a meeting with the vicar of that parish, a tour of the parish and perhaps meeting one or two other senior local church figures. In this meeting you're both trying to feel out what each other is like, whether you could work together, whether the parish is somewhere you could live and be happy for three or four years. If the first meeting goes well and you think you make a pretty good fit there might be a couple of follow-up meetings, perhaps meeting more of the church officials from the parish and taking a look at the curate's accommodation they're offering. If the parish likes what they see, they'll send a letter to the bishop, officially offering you a place there as their curate. In response, if you like what you see, you'll write back, officially accepting the place. And Bob's your uncle.

What if they don't like you? Or you don't like them?

It happens a lot. Either side is free to say 'thanks, but no thanks' at any stage. If this happens, it's back to the drawing board. If the diocese has another free parish to offer, you might be sent another profile. If they don't, then you're released, and you are back to checking out the pile of parish profiles waiting at your theological college.

I should say that both sides of this equation should only be looking at one option at a time. Parishes aren't supposed to have a squad of ordinand candidates competing to be their curate, and at the same time, ordinands aren't supposed to have more than one potential parish on the go. This is to avoid the obvious manipulation that could result, with people being played off against one another. Sadly, the fact is that both of these things do happen in reality. It makes looking for that first curacy one of the most stressful times in an ordinand's training. Wander round a theological college in early autumn when most people are actively looking for a curacy and the tension will be palpable.

So you've got a place to be a curate. What then?

The vicar or rector of the parish where you've become the new curate has a responsibility to train you. They're known as your 'training incumbent'. Different training incumbents do this in different ways. Some like you to follow them around just watching what they do for a while before striking out on your own. Some like to sit you down and tell you what the job's about. On the other hand, some like to throw you into the deep end and see if you'll swim. With any luck you'll have asked the right questions at your 'get to know you' meetings and will both know and get on with your trainer's teaching style. Of course, this isn't always the case, and can be the cause of a lot of tension between vicar and curate.

Once you've got the go-ahead, though, curacies are all about learning by doing. You do all the things the vicar does and get better by practising. So, in your first year, you're a deacon. You can do everything except blessing, declaring God's forgiveness ('absolving') and presiding at services of Holy Communion. So that's what you do. You lead prayers, you preach, you take funerals, you visit sick and needy people and you take a hand in whatever else is going on in your parish. This varies from place to place. Your parish might be big on working with other faith groups, or on organising the various local Christian churches to do things together, or on working in schools or with young people, or on projects to help the homeless ... or any number of other things.

After a year, if everything is going well, you'll usually be ordained priest. The bishop decides who will be 'priested' based on an annual review process which happens a few months before decisions need to be made. Once you have been priested you get to do everything else that your vicar does in the parish. So you lead Holy Communion services, you take weddings and baptisms and you can bless and absolve. For the next two to three years you do all these things, along with all the things you were doing as a deacon.

That all sounds very ad hoc. How does anyone know if you're doing well or not?

Ah yes. That's the tricky bit. The diocese wants to know that you've been properly trained. Come to that, you want to know that you've been properly trained. Once your curacy is up you'll be out in the big wide world, perhaps taking responsibility for a whole parish, and you need to know you're up to snuff. To help with this, the House of Bishops have put together a long list of things that you are expected to be, or to have done, or to be able to do, by the end of your curacy.

Everyone has an annual review process, where you report on your successes and failures over the year, and set goals for the year ahead. But apart from this, different dioceses measure your progress in different ways. Some like you to take another degree as a test of learning. Some like you to record your learning progress in a portfolio or through a journalling process. In Oxford, where I am, we produce a 'Ministry Development Folder'. In this we collate evidence that shows we've learned what the bishops want us to learn. This evidence might be through essays we've written (and we all have to write a certain number of these), or pieces of written feedback we've got from our training incumbent or other senior members of our parish, or it might be through journal-type reflections we've written. When we think we've hit all the targets the bishops set down, and have put the evidence together in our folders, they get sent off to be marked. To finish our curacies, an assessor needs to decide we have indeed learned all we're supposed to have done, based on the evidence we've put together.

Once we've been judged to have matched up to the bishops' expectations our training is officially over and we're free to go out and start working on our own.

The job

How much control do you have over where you work? Do you just go wherever you're sent?

No! You're the one in control. Different dioceses have different ways of handling priests looking to move on, but in every case you find what jobs are available, you decide which of those you might fit, and you apply for them. You can do this in a variety of different ways: talking to your bishop, or the bishop of the diocese to which you'd like to move; talking to the archdeacon in the area you'd like to be; hooking into the clergy grapevine to see which positions might be likely to be free in the near future; giving your name to the Clergy Appointments Advisor in London who circulates a list of clergy looking for posts to the various dioceses; or simply by checking out adverts posted in the church press. Once you've found a likely option, you apply.

So what does applying involve?

If you're going for a place in a 'normal' parish (i.e. not a chaplaincy or something similar), this usually involves filling out a standard application form along with a CV and covering letter. If you've got what the parish is looking for, you'll get onto the shortlist for interviewing. An interview will usually be you facing a panel consisting of either the bishop or archdeacon, the 'patron' of the parish or their representative and two parish representatives who have been elected by their Parochial Church Council. These two reps have the right of veto over candidates. There are often several rounds of interviews, depending on how many people applied for the position and the quality of the applicants.

'Patron'? 'Parochial Church Council'?

A patron is a family or college or organisation which has a vested interest in the parish. They might own the land the church is built on, for example, or they might have originally paid for the church to be built. Many churches' patrons are Oxford or Cambridge colleges. The church where I currently serve finds its patron in the head of the family whose estate historically included the land the church is built upon.

The Parochial Church Council, or PCC as it's usually known, formally represents the laity in a church and deals with the general running of the church. Its members are elected by the congregation and make decisions on everything from which weekend the church fête should to be held to whether to spend money on reorganising the entire interior of the church. The vicar is a member of the PCC and traditionally will chair it as well. Needless to say, a good relationship with the PCC is essential for a vicar.

What's the pay like?

Low. And every vicar gets the same amount, wherever you work, whatever you do. Vicars who are paid by the Church are known as 'stipendiary' clergy in that they receive a 'stipend' from the Church Commissioners, the group in charge of the finances of the whole Church of England. There are also plenty of serving priests and deacons who are not paid, but they will usually be either retired or self-supported by working in another job, so will not be vicars – they won't be in charge of a parish.

All that said, at time of writing the stipend for a full-time stipendiary cleric is around £21k a year before tax.

But don't you get a house too?

This is true. Clerics employed within parishes are provided with housing, and the upkeep of the property is the responsibility of the PCC in question. If you're working outside a parish context, however, for example as a chaplain or educator, the house may not necessarily be part of the deal.

Do vicars get all kinds of tax breaks?

Sadly not. We get to claim necessary expenses, and have an allowance for heating, lighting and cleaning, since our homes are also our workplaces, but that's all pretty standard for anyone working from home.

When there's a collection in church, does the vicar get it?

No! That is strictly forbidden. All collections have to be counted with at least two people present, and then they are paid into the parish's account. From this central account the parish has to pay a designated sum to the diocese every year (designated according to how many paid clergy the parish has and how many people attend the church) which will then be used and redistributed in the form of clergy stipends. The collection thus goes mainly to pay clergy stipends, then to pay for the upkeep of the church buildings, including heating, lighting and the fabric of the church, then to pay for other church projects, and finally to be distributed to chosen charities.

Any extra money that may come the way of the clergy (collections, fees for marriages and funerals, etc.) has to be declared and either paid into the parish funds or returned to the diocese.

Are you allowed to get married?

Yes. Thankfully the Church of England is absolutely fine with its vicars being and getting married. My husband is glad to hear it.

Do you get holidays?

Yes. I get six weeks annual leave in a year. The conditions are that I can only have six Sundays off in a year and I must work during the major Christian festivals – Christmas and Easter. Vicars are encouraged to take one of those weeks' holiday immediately after Christmas and another after Easter. The big festivals really burn you out, so you need the time to recharge.

Is it ok for you to be into strange things like science fiction? Are the powers that be happy with that?

Yes, it's fine, and a great many vicars of my acquaintance enjoy reading/watching the odd bit of science fiction. My twitter stream is full of clergy rhapsodising about the latest *Doctor Who* episode. It's almost expected that vicars will have at least one quirky thing that makes them unique. It might be a love of science fiction. It might be enjoying getting dressed in Dark Age armour and re-enacting major battles of the period. It might be practising martial arts. It might be collecting Japanese anime and manga. It might be playing bass in a rhythm and blues band. Or in my case, it might be all of those things.

Can you turn undead and smack things with maces?

One for the D&D fans out there (if you don't know what that is, ignore this question). No to the maces. As for the first part … it depends what you mean. One part of the vicars' day-to-day work involves interacting with peoples' hopes and fears about the supernatural and what happens after death. As a result there is a certain amount of visiting and praying in homes that the residents believe are home to restless spirits. More on this later.

Do you have to like tea?

It doesn't hurt, although it's acceptable to ask for coffee instead. But it's certainly true that when you visit people, 'Would you like some tea?' often the first question you're asked. I'm told if it's the right time of day and there's not much going on later a bold vicar might even ask for a beer. I've not been bold enough to do this yet.

How long can vicars carry on working for?

These days the retirement age for clergy is 70 years old, although that is almost certain to change again before long. Even after retirement, though, as long as a priest has 'permission to officiate', given by the bishop, they can keep ministering for as long as they are able to do so. Some priests even take up a 'house for duty', which means they aren't paid a salary, but are given a place to live in return for putting in a minimum amount of hours with the local church.

Do you have to do some kind of continuing training or study?

Yes. Vicars have a regular review process administered by
the diocese, and they need to show how they have been
continuing their training and study. Training might be specific
seminars or courses, but it may equally well just mean that the
vicar is keeping up their theological reading.

*What do you do and how far can you go as a vicar if you disagree
with church policy?*

The Church of England is pretty open and flexible as far as
religious institutions go. It contains a wide variety of different
stances, interpretations and practices as long as the core
beliefs are held in common. This means that nailing down
precisely what 'church policy' consists of isn't an easy task.
Indeed, the Church is always in motion (although often not at
the speed more progressive believers might wish) as we learn
more about what God wants from us and we understand more
about ourselves and the world. Policy isn't static.

   Which is a long-winded way of saying that if you disagree
with the current status quo as a vicar it's not necessarily a
problem, or something that will hold you back. There's a grand
tradition of making changes from the inside, and many vicars
take this prophetic role to heart, criticising the institution
and encouraging church government to move in different
directions. As always though, there is a fine line between
being seen as an agitator for change and being seen as disloyal.
Be too vocal and you might find yourself pushed aside. The
Church is a human institution, after all, and other human
institutions are no different.

   The exception to this general rule of flexibility is if you
break church law, which is laid down in black and white in
what are called the Canons of the Church. Let's take views
on homosexuality as an example. Among vicars you'll find the
whole spread of opinions about homosexuality. This is fine.
But currently the Church forbids services of blessing for same-

sex partnerships. If a vicar flaunts this rule, they might get into trouble, depending on the views of their bishop.

What are you actually trying to be and do? Do you think you're some kind of spiritual warrior? A teacher? Just someone who reads out sermons on a Sunday? What?

To be honest, a vicar is a bit of a jack of all trades. You have to be passably good at a great many different things. Teaching, public speaking, counselling, listening, chairing meetings, leading worship, praying … The list goes on. Most vicars will be excellent at a couple of these, pretty good at most of the rest, and absolutely rubbish at at least one. The trick is knowing what you're rubbish at and making sure that whatever it is can be looked after by someone who isn't rubbish at it.

As for what vicars think they are, that's hard to say because everyone is different. There may well be some vicars out there who do indeed feel themselves to be spiritual warriors. I can only really speak for myself. I think there's something of a teacher in me, but the heart of what I'm trying to be is a representative. I'm trying to represent God's love for his people – to show it in how I interact with people, with what I teach them about God and the Bible, and in how I lead worship and prayer. And at the same time I need to represent the people to whom I'm a spiritual leader back to God. I pray for them, and I recognise and embrace our shared humanity.

I would love to be a spiritual warrior. I'd love to be a Jedi-like figure, knowledgeable and wise, and able literally to fight for the forces of light and goodness. But the world isn't so clearly good and bad. I'm not sure who or what I'd be trying to fight!

The gear

What do you wear day to day?

Okay, first thing to say is that not all vicars wear the same stuff. When we're not leading worship, some vicars wear jeans and a T-shirt, some wear black clerical shirts and all-black suits. It depends on the tradition you follow – what is sometimes called 'high churchmanship' or 'low churchmanship'. I'll talk more about church traditions in the section on the modern Church of England.

I'm from a 'middle of the road' tradition, so I usually wear smart jeans or trousers with clerical shirts of varying dark colours – black, navy, dark green etc.

What's a clerical shirt?

One of those shirts with a 'dog collar' at the throat .

'Dog collar'?

That strip of white at the collar that you see on vicars. Needless to say, it's not officially known as a 'dog collar', but in practice you'll find that most clergy use this affectionate nickname for it. The proper name is a 'clerical collar'.

There are three main types of clerical collar. The most common is the 'slip-in', where you just have that flash of white where the top button of the shirt would be. But you can also get shirt collar versions, where it looks like you've just shoved a piece of white plastic under a normal shirt collar, and 'tonsure' versions, where there is the usual thick strip of white at the throat, but there is also a thin strip of white visible above the shirt material all around the neck. Again, which type you choose will say something about the church tradition from which you come.

I wear slip-in collars most of the time, and tonsure collars on occasions when I have to look extra smart.

Is it true that you could make a dog collar from a Fairy Liquid bottle?

Back when the bottles were made of white plastic, yes you could. I've not personally known any vicars to do this, but I'm sure one or two have done it in the past. Actually the white plastic that makes the dog collar comes with the shirt. I've got a drawer full of them.

What's a cassock, then? I thought vicars wore those?

Vicars do wear them, but generally only when leading worship. Although some church traditions have vicars wearing cassocks all the time, that's pretty rare. A cassock is that long black robe-like garment that goes all the way from your neck down to the tops of your shoes. Some button up the front, some are double-breasted – again, it's a church tradition thing.

Does wearing the dog collar make you behave differently?

Not terribly, to be honest. Certainly being ordained made a change in how I see myself, and often in how I act, but whether I'm wearing the collar or not I still feel what it represents, if that makes sense. I wish it had magic properties, like make me into a better driver, but it doesn't, and I still devolve when I get behind the wheel. I'm sure it's not a vicar-like quality to shout at other drivers for failing to signal at roundabouts, but if I'm driving the car it happens.

What it does change is how people see me. You get used to people staring at you on the street for a start. Sometimes it makes people more talkative, sometimes it makes them avoid you like the plague. If I'm wearing the collar on public transport it's not often that someone will sit in an empty seat next to me. I don't know what they think I'm going to do! Some vicars of my acquaintance get angrily shouted at when they're out in their collars, but thankfully that's not happened to me yet. Where you are makes a big difference in that, I think.

So what do you wear when you're taking a service?

You'll get bored of hearing this, but it depends on your church tradition. Church law says you have to wear either a cassock, surplice and tippet (also known more simply as a preaching scarf), or an alb and stole. In 'higher' church circles, there will also be other vestments worn over the top of the alb and stole, such as a chasuble or dalmatic.

A what, a what and a what?

Don't panic! I'll get to those in a minute. In practice though, if you're from a more 'evangelical' church tradition you might not wear anything more special than a suit and tie when you lead worship. Church lawyers would take you to task about it if they found out, but to be honest nobody else worries too much.

So what do all those strange names mean?

First of all is the cassock, surplice, preaching scarf ensemble. A surplice is worn over the top of a cassock, and is a wide-sleeved baggy white shirt-like garment that usually comes down to the knees. The look is topped off with the preaching scarf – a long black scarf that goes around the neck without being tied and hangs down to around knee level on either side. You'll wear this if you're from a more evangelical church tradition, or if you're leading worship that doesn't involve Holy Communion, such as morning or evening prayer. This ensemble is known as 'choir dress', and if you want, you can add your academic degree hood to show your theological qualifications.

And the alb and stole?

You wear these at services involving Holy Communion, although many vicars will wear them at weddings and funerals as well. An alb is a long white robe-like garment that, like a cassock, goes all the way from your neck down to your shoes. It can either be of a thinner material that is worn over the top of a cassock, or of a thicker material (making it into a 'cassock-alb') that just goes over your normal clothes. A stole is a scarf-like garment which is wide and flat, and usually decorated with embroidery. If you're from a more catholic tradition this will usually be made of brocade, and embroidered in gold. Other traditions will use various materials and embroidery, ranging from the very simple to the hugely elaborate.

While a preaching scarf is always black, clergy wear stoles coloured for the church seasons. So you will have stoles in the following colours: white or gold, red, purple and green. Some clergy will have black ones as well for funerals, but that's much rarer.

One final thing about stoles – they are worn in different ways according to whether you're a priest or a deacon. Deacons wear their stoles like sashes, diagonally across the body, fastened on the right hip. Priests wear them like preaching scarves, hanging around the neck with the ends parallel and coming down to around knee-level.

And those other things? Chasuble and dalmatic?

A chasuble is worn over the top of the alb and stole by priests of higher church traditions when presiding at services of Holy Communion. It's a garment usually made of silk brocade and heavily embroidered that looks and wears a bit like a poncho. Like the stole, the chasuble is coloured for the church season, and priests and churches will often purchase matching chasuble and stole sets.

A dalmatic is not in use as much as a chasuble, but can be worn by a deacon serving at Holy Communion services. It's a long, wide-sleeved tunic, again made of brocade and embroidered, that goes over the top of the alb and stole.

What's the significance of the things you wear? Do they mean anything?

Some more than others. Let's start with the dog collar itself.

Dog collar: Better called a clerical collar if you want to avoid strangers staring at you while you talk about clerical wear. These days, Church of England clergy of all levels (deacon, priest, bishop) wear clerical collars to show that they're ordained. But the look actually comes from the nineteenth century when clergymen (and of course they were *men* back then) would wear white silk stocks (like a cravat – think Mr Darcy in *Pride and Prejudice*) that would protrude over the top of their long black coats. In the modern Church this look is re-created with a specially made collar and a piece of white plastic.

Cassock: The name 'cassock' derives from the French *casaque* meaning a long coat, and that's just what a cassock was originally. It was simply smart outer wear for clergy. These days of course it goes under the surplice as part of choir dress. There are two versions in the Church of England. One is double breasted, fastening at the shoulders, and is known as 'Sarum style'. The other is single breasted, buttoning from the top to the bottom. This is often worn by those from higher church traditions, and will usually fasten with 39 buttons, symbolising the 39 Articles of Religion ratified by the infant Church of England in 1571. That's as symbolic as it gets though.

Surplice: The surplice, along with cassock and preaching scarf, forms choir dress, the clerical wear prescribed by the Church of England since the mid-sixteenth century for deacons and priests leading worship. It was originally an ankle-length garment, but shortened over the centuries until it hit the knee-length version generally worn today. As with the alb, the significance of the surplice is its colour. It's white, denoting purity, and is a concealing garment, supposed to hide the person and personal style of the individual cleric.

There's also a super-short hip-length version of the surplice called a cotta. This is sometimes decorated with lace, and is usually worn by clerics from an Anglo-Catholic church tradition.

Preaching scarf (tippet): Again, this evolved over time from the original fashion. So instead of the long baggy black sleeves that would have been around before the fourteenth century, they have become the long black scarf that modern clergy wear. Alternatively it could be argued that the scarf is derived from the stripes signifying rank on a Roman toga or as a symbol of learning in the early church age. However, there's no modern theological significance. The scarf simply distinguishes the wearer as someone ordained in the Church.

Alb: The term comes from the Latin *albus* meaning white. Historically this ankle-length garment would have been the tunic worn by Romans. Its significance, like the surplice, is its colour and concealing nature. In more middle-of-the-road church traditions the alb is often combined with the cassock as a 'cassock-alb'. This is white, but made of heavier material than an alb. In more Anglo-Catholic traditions, the alb is often worn with an 'amice', a white neck scarf tied under the alb to protect the collar from the back of the neck. The amice is said to symbolise the 'helmet of salvation' in Paul's letter to the Ephesians (Ephesians 6:10–17).

Cincture: This is the rope belt that clergy often wear to bring the alb in at the waist. It's symbolic of the 'belt of truth' in a reading from Ephesians.

Stole: The stole was originally a large shawl, worn over the shoulders, which is why its name comes from the Greek *stol* meaning a garment. Over the centuries, it reduced in size into the long, narrow strip of cloth it is now. Symbolically it is often linked with the 'yoke of Christ', a reference to Jesus asking people to take on his yoke in Matthew 11:29. It's also linked to the towel Jesus tied around himself when he washed the disciples' feet, and the bonds he was tied with in his last days.

Chasuble: This started life as outer wear as well. The term is from the Latin *casula* – 'little house'. Originally it was very like a poncho, simply an oval of material with a hole in the middle.

It's got more stylised over the years, but the basic form has remained the same. Symbolically the chasuble is a reminder of the 'seamless garment' Jesus wore on the way to the cross.

Dalmatic: This was originally a formal over-tunic in Roman times. It doesn't have any particular symbolic meaning.

The day to day

Do you only work on Sundays?

No. Oh dear. If I had a pound for every time somebody said this I'd be rolling in cash. No, decidedly not. Sundays are for services. One of my two churches has four services on a Sunday, for example. It also has a service on a Wednesday morning. Other churches might have services every single day of the week. But leading worship in services is only a tiny fraction of what a vicar actually does.

Do you have to work weekends?

Yes. Sundays are obviously a big work day, but Saturdays are when the majority of weddings happen, and when people of working age are at home to be visited. Saturdays are definitely work days.

So do you get time off in the week?

We get one day a week off. The day you take can vary. Most vicars take their day off on a Friday, because it gives you a chance to catch your breath before what is usually a busy weekend. I take mine on a Thursday. We're also generally encouraged to make sure the evening of the previous day is also free, to maximise the downtime. This is sometimes possible and sometimes really not.

I should say that this is only theoretical. The Church urges vicars to make sure that they really do take a day off a week

as well as all our annual leave. In practice, many vicars don't.
There may be no one to take over duties for them while they
take a holiday, or emergencies keep coming up on their day off,
and before they know it, they're working 7 days a week, 365
days a year. Needless to say, this isn't a good idea, and leads to
a high level of vicar burnout.

Vicar burnout?

Sadly, yes. A surprisingly high proportion of new vicars work
themselves to burnout and breakdowns. The work of a vicar
never really stops, and it's for results that might not appear
for years, or might not be visible at all. Plus vicars have to
deal with isolation (many vicars are on their own in their
parish) and a great deal of pressure from the expectations
that surround them. The Church is working very hard at the
moment to try to make sure vicars don't drive themselves too
hard and have systems in place to take care of themselves and
de-stress. I suppose we'll see whether this has worked over
the next decade or so.

What does an average working day look like?

Well, there's not really an average day in a vicar's life. The only
really predictable days are Sundays, because then at least you
know the services will be at the same time every week. Here's
what one of my more predictable days (Monday) looks like
though:

> 7:00–07:30 – Morning Prayer. This is a 20-minute service,
> and happens in the church. There's no music, which is
> just as well since singing at that hour of the morning is a
> non-starter for me. Instead it consists a simple collection
> of Bible readings and prayers.

> 7:30–08:30 – Desk work. I might go over the assembly
> due to happen at 9 a.m., check my diary for the day

and week ahead, or prepare a simple report for the staff meeting later.

8:30 – Greeting at the school gate. My training incumbent and I make a habit of standing at the local church primary school gate on a Monday morning to greet the parents and children. It's a good chance for people to have a word with us if they need to, and it makes us approachable and visible.

9:00 – School assembly. We always take the church primary school assembly on a Monday morning. It takes about 15 minutes to speak to the 200 or so pupils.

9:30 – Staff meeting. This is an hour or so, sharing news with our youth worker colleagues, making plans for the week ahead and making sure we all know what's going on in the life of the church in the near future.

10:30–12:00 – This time is open. I usually use it for desk-based paperwork. This can be making sure my expenses are up to date, answering emails, making phone calls, or working on sermons.

12:00–13:00 – Lunch!

13:00–18:00 – This is where the variety comes into things. Monday afternoons could contain many things. Here's a list of what might be happening:

- Pastoral visiting. This is paying visits to anyone who needs it. This could just be touching base with parishioners, but more usually it's bringing comfort to the sick, housebound, lonely and those in spiritual need. Often it's bringing blessed bread and wine to those Christians who want to share in Holy Communion, but aren't able to leave their homes or hospital beds.
- Funeral visits. This is spending an hour or so with the bereaved family and/or friends to discuss what they would like for the funeral service and to simply share

their memories of their lost loved one. For whatever reason, my parish gets a lot of funerals, so these visits are a regular part of my week.

- Baptism preparation. This is as it sounds, visiting the family of the person to be baptised and getting them up to speed with what happens at the service and what it might mean to them.
- Marriage preparation. Similarly, this is a visit to the happy couple, finding out what they would like at their wedding and doing some teaching about how the Church understands marriage.
- Funerals. Funerals can happen any day of the week (although usually not Sunday), and at any time from about 10 a.m. to 5 p.m.
- Meetings. Vicars often have a hand in the community projects in their parish. So there's a need to attend plenty of meetings with community youth workers, council officials, other faith leaders, housing projects and so on.
- Leading worship. Although my church generally worships in the morning, or in the evening as well on a Sunday, I will periodically lead worship that happens in the afternoon or evening, such as with the youth group or Mothers' Union.
- Studying. This might be for something specific, like writing a sermon or some other publication, but vicars are also supposed to keep up with their theological study. More on this in a bit.
- Praying. This might sound odd to non-Christians, but vicars need to pray a lot. A vicar who doesn't have a healthy relationship with God, mediated through prayer, isn't going to be much help to their congregation.

18:00–19:00 – Dinner!

19:00–22:00 – This is usually downtime for me. But from time to time there'll be something that has to happen in the evening, like a PCC meeting, or a marriage or baptism preparation session with families that can only meet in the evening.

There's also the possibility of emergencies at any point in the day. If someone is dying and wants the vicar there, for example, we would drop everything to get there. And 'everything' really does mean everything.

Do you need to prioritise? Is pastoral work more important than church services, for example?

You do need to prioritise, because there just isn't time in the day to do everything. And as new things come in there's a need to reprioritise on a startlingly regular basis. Some things are fixed, like taking school assemblies or leading church services, which makes them straightforward, because everything else fits in around them. It doesn't make them more important than the other things, it just means that they can only be where they are.

The hard part is deciding what to do with the open time. Which sick person needs visiting more urgently? Is it more important to write Sunday's sermon or to take some time to pray? It's tough. Some things take immediate priority, like things with a very short deadline, or which can only happen at certain times. Funeral visits are the best example of this kind of thing. You'll generally only have a week in which to visit the bereaved before the funeral, and the timing depends on when they are free. Your schedule has to be shifted around them.

Similarly, very ill people go straight to the top of the list. One of the things they try to teach you in training is to use your time well, and not to neglect things that you need. If prayer and study end up *continually* being pushed to the bottom of your to-do list and thus never get done, you're not doing anyone any favours.

Do all clergy wait until late on Saturday night before preparing the Sunday sermon?

Well I'm afraid it's true in my case, at least the actual writing the thing down. But not for all vicars, thank goodness. I know some vicars who are tremendously organised and write their sermons well in advance. Last-minute sermon writing is both a blessing and a curse. If something major that needs to be talked about happens late in the week, you're perfectly placed to include it in your sermon. But it does put a strain on Saturday night, especially if you're lacking in inspiration. In the end I think it's down to your personality.

What do you want to achieve with sermons?

Sermons can serve all kinds of different purposes. As a preacher, my ultimate aim is to communicate whatever God wants to say to his people that week. That may sound a bit wishy-washy, but it's more concrete than that. I believe that God always has something special he wants me to say to his congregation.

How do you prepare? How long does it take to write?

When I prepare a sermon I will read the Bible readings for the service a few days in advance and let them soak in. I will pray around them, do some background research about their context – who wrote them, when, why and so on – and just become comfortable with them. Then I will pray about the things happening in the world that week, about the things that might be happening in the congregation, and ask for guidance. Usually I will be guided to a series of connections between readings and what the congregation have on their minds, and that will form the basis of the sermon. The original reading and research usually takes a couple of hours for each sermon. The writing itself takes two to three hours.

Sermons can do a lot. They can be used to teach, to encourage, to explain, or to challenge. One week I might want to remind the congregation about the Christian call to look after the natural world, another week I might want to comfort

them as they deal with the serious illness of a much-loved
member of the community. When something big happens
in the public consciousness, like the Parliamentary expenses
scandal, or the Boston bombing or an attention-grabbing
criminal trial, I will often try to address that with my sermon.
It's important that the congregation's Christian faith is applied
to what's happening in the world and in their everyday lives
on a regular basis, otherwise it becomes nothing more than a
story we tell each other on Sundays.

The hardest stuff

*What do you do when people talk about suicidal thoughts in
confession?*

In my church tradition there's not much call for confession, but
it does happen.

First and most importantly, in all questions regarding
confession, a clear distinction needs to be drawn between
pastoral conversation and confession itself. Although a pastoral
conversation may be of a confidential nature, under the
Human Rights Act the priest would be permitted to disclose
details of harm done to others, whether that harm is already
done or is planned for the future.

However, the House of Bishops' advice is that if we're
talking about the formal rite of confession, rather than simply
a pastoral conversation, the confidentiality of the confession
is absolute (although in law there are a few exceptions which
I'll get to in a moment). In the rite of confession, someone
(the 'penitent') will confess their thoughts and wrongdoings
to the priest one-to-one, and the priest then declares God's
forgiveness. The priest is then bound not to reveal anything
of what has been said. So if someone talked about suicidal
thoughts in confession, I would be bound to keep that
between us. I could, however, strongly encourage that person
to seek help, to the extent of calling mental health emergency
lines right then and there if the person agreed to it.

Sometimes when people talk about suicidal thoughts they are nowhere near actually committing suicide. But occasionally that's not the case. If I was seriously concerned that the person was going to act on their suicidal thoughts and they were refusing to seek help, I might ask someone else to check in on them, without revealing any details or why I was asking them to do so. That way I would have kept the integrity of the confessional, but would not be abandoning someone in pain when they needed help.

What about if people talk about harming others in confession?

In such cases the advice from the House of Bishops remains the same, that is, that the confidentiality of confession should be absolute. The priest's first response should be to advise the person to turn themselves in to the authorities. If they refuse, the situation becomes more difficult. The priest would begin by acting on the fact that in the rite of confession the priest can withhold absolution, or make absolution conditional on certain actions. So the priest can encourage the confessing person to turn themselves into the police, or to seek mental health assistance from social services, and this encouragement can go all the way up to withholding forgiveness until the person reports their actions or intent. That is, make declaring God's forgiveness conditional upon the person reporting their actions to the police.

If the person isn't persuaded by this, the legal situation is cloudy. As elsewhere, the priest has no legal requirement to report a crime or intent to commit a crime, although I'd suggest there is a strong moral requirement to do so, particularly when the 'other' in question is a child. In addition, if the priest refuses to give evidence against the penitent as a witness in court, they may be held in contempt of court and sentenced accordingly.

Current advice from the House of Bishops is that in cases where the person refuses to turn themselves in to the authorities even when absolution is made conditional or entirely withheld, the priest can, and indeed should, speak to their bishop and alert the bishop to what is happening, although the penitent's name and details cannot be passed on without their permission. The priest might also encourage the penitent to speak personally to the bishop.

All that said, there are a number of things that may not be covered by the seal of the confessional. Among these are treason, terrorism and money laundering. If a penitent were to confess any of these three crimes, or the intent to carry them out, the priest could and should disclose what they have heard to the authorities, whether or not the penitent hands themselves in.

How hard is it to keep emotionally detached and concentrate on the job in tough situations?

When I was first ordained, I was terrified that when I spoke to bereaved people and took funerals I would dissolve into tears. I've always been moved by other people's emotions, and would always be in floods at funerals. So I was surprised to discover that when I was in these situations as a deacon and later as a priest, I was in no danger of breaking down. It's probably something about being in a 'professional' state of mind. I also firmly believe that God supports me and helps me to be a support for those who need me in those situations.

Sure, there are some super-hard situations. I took the funeral of a baby girl who lived for only 36 minutes recently. I was six months pregnant at the time. Trying not to break down during that funeral, especially when her dad placed the tiny vessel containing her ashes into the ground, was the hardest it's ever been for me.

Vicars and culture

How do you feel about how vicars have been sent up in comedy?

It's frustrating and fun in equal measure. It's a good sign that vicars are held in enough affectionate regard that comedians might want to send us up. It means we're part of everyday life and considered fair game for a laugh. I like that, and there are some really funny vicar-related jokes and skits out there that absolutely let rip.

At the same time it can be a bit frustrating, in that people know more about the stereotype than the reality, and the two get confused. But then I suppose that's always how things work. I'm glad for the comedies out there that manage to be affectionate, funny and real. *The Vicar of Dibley* and the wonderful *Rev* are two great examples.

Are you ever tempted to use vicar status to claim an expertise (in ethics/life etc.) when arguing?

Not so far. I don't think it's an acceptable way to behave for starters, and, besides, there might have been a time when the status of a vicar was such that you could try to pull rank in that kind of way, but a vicar's status just isn't like that any more. Being a vicar isn't something that immediately gives someone expertise. Vicars earn expertise like anyone else, and we stand or fall on the strength of our arguments, not on whether we have the right to wear a dog collar or not.

The Church of England: Past and present

The past

Beginnings

Was Jesus the actual founder of Christianity?

The short answer is yes. I'll deal with what vicars believe in that section, but for now, take it as read that we believe Jesus was a real person who lived in first-century Palestine, was crucified by the Romans, died, but after three days rose from the dead.

Before he was crucified, Jesus gathered a large group of people around him who followed him around the country as he taught and healed people. Twelve of the men (the 'disciples') and four of the women are named in the Bible (although a couple of the names change from Gospel to Gospel), but the Gospels make it clear that there were more than that in the group as a whole. After Jesus died, rose and then departed into heaven, it was this group of people who spread the word about who Jesus was and had been, and who organised themselves into the beginnings of the church we know today.

Jesus didn't write a book. Rather, he brought people together and changed their lives. The Church isn't the institution or the buildings or the doctrine. It's the people who ended up calling themselves Christians.

What's a 'Gospel'?

It's the name we give to the first four books of the New Testament: the Gospels of Matthew, Mark, Luke and John. These are the books in which we are told the story of Jesus' life, death and resurrection, as opposed to the other books of the New Testament which consist of a history of the very early Church, a collection of letters to and from various people, and a recounting of a vision. 'Gospel' is an Old English word, literally meaning 'good news'.

Was the Church back then very different from the one we see now?

Yes. Because it hadn't acquired all the baggage that we have now, after two thousand years. Baggage which includes, it has to be said, all the awfulness the Church still carries around – like the legacy of the many terrible crimes committed in the name of Christianity through the centuries.

That first Church was small. It was made up purely of Jews, who were quite secure in their Jewish identity. As far as they were concerned, Jesus was the figure prophesied in their holy scriptures, and as good Jews they should live new lives as he taught them. The story of the earliest Church is recorded in the fifth book of the New Testament – the Acts of the Apostles. In the earliest days they all lived in Palestine, with most of them in its capital Jerusalem, and continued to worship with other Jews in synagogues and in the Temple. The difference was that they also continued to talk about Jesus.

At that point in history there were lots of Jewish groups or sects that were setting themselves up as 'proper' Judaism. The Essene sect is a good example. Its members were the ones who gave us the Dead Sea Scrolls. They were Jews who thought 'proper' Judaism meant not only keeping the Jewish law and worshipping the one true God, but also an extreme asceticism – self-denial, purity and isolation from the 'polluting' influence of outsiders. In addition they had a new calendar and a new interpretation of the Law that meant they felt they could no longer worship with mainstream Judaism in a Temple

they viewed as defiled. So they broke away from Jewish
society as a whole and set up their own communities.

The bunch of people who had followed Jesus around while
he was alive were seen as, and started out as, more of the same.

The church was Jewish? When did that change?

It was a gradual thing, although the Christ-followers' move
away from Judaism was more or less complete by 100 CE or so.
Other Jewish groups, particularly the priestly hierarchy and
the educated experts in the Jewish Law, the Sadducees and
the Pharisees, pushed hard against what they thought were
Jewish heretics. There was a fair amount of persecution, with
early followers of Jesus being killed and imprisoned.

At the same time, early Christ-followers began to spread
the story of Jesus much further afield, including to non-Jews.
We know this because some of the letters written by one of
the most famous early Christ-followers were preserved by
the Church and included in the Bible. Paul of Tarsus wrote his
letters in the period of around 45 to 60 CE (dating depending
on the letter and which scholar you talk to), and in them and
in Acts you can see the story of how his journeys around the
Mediterranean seeded a number of small Christ-following
communities made up of both Jews and non-Jews.

CE?

These days theologians and Biblical scholars try not to use the
dating terms AD (Anno Domini) and BC (Before Christ) because
of the cultural assumptions they carry with them. Instead we
use CE (Common Era) and BCE (Before Common Era). They
refer to exactly the same time frames. So, for example, AD 33
is exactly the same as 33 CE.

Sounds like that wouldn't have been an easy break.

It wasn't. For a start, Jews follow the Law as laid down in
the first five books of the Bible: Genesis, Exodus, Leviticus,

Numbers and Deuteronomy, which the Jews call the *Torah*. It
includes lists of things you can and can't eat, special rituals you
have to follow on certain occasions, and the fact that Jewish
men must be circumcised eight days after birth.

Non-Jews hearing about Jesus wanted to follow him and
join this new group, but plenty of them didn't want to take
on all the Jewish trappings as well. They didn't want to be
circumcised or follow these complicated food laws. As far as
they were concerned, surely it was enough that they were
living their lives as Jesus wanted them to?

There were tremendous rows about it. Paul was on the
side of the non-Jewish Christians, saying that what you ate
or whether or not you were circumcised should make no
difference at all. Peter and others like him back in Jerusalem,
notably the leader of the Jerusalem Christ-followers, James
the brother of Jesus, felt differently. They felt they should be
Jews first.

So how was that worked out?

Two things. Firstly, the Jerusalem Christ-followers found
themselves in the middle of a war zone when radical Jewish
forces revolted against Roman rule in 66 CE and slaughtered
the Sadducees and the Temple elite for being Roman
collaborators. Unsurprisingly, the Romans didn't take kindly
to this, poured resources into crushing the rebels, and in the
process the Temple was burned down. The Jerusalem Christ-
followers' response was to get out of there as quickly as
possible, and flee elsewhere. The fact that they were outside
the capital, and under pressure from other Jews for not taking
sides in the Jews versus Romans war, meant they lost a great
deal of influence and prestige. In effect they slowly faded
away.

Secondly, the war meant the Sadducees were all dead
and the Pharisees were the strongest party left in Judaism.
Their influence meant what it was to be Jewish became much
narrower, and the old pattern of strong regional variations
disappeared. Christ-followers couldn't fit in with a mish-mash

of different understandings of 'Jewishness' any more. They were something distinctively different.

Eventually the followers of Jesus stopped thinking of themselves as Jews at all, but it was a painful shift.

You keep calling them 'Christ-followers'. Didn't they call themselves Christians?

Not in the beginning. 'Christian' was a Latin nickname (and not a fond one) they acquired in Antioch, a slang term using the word 'Christ' – *Christiani*. It might be translated, as biblical scholar Professor K. C. Hanson does, 'Christ-niks'. 'Christ' itself is a Greek translation of the Hebrew term 'Messiah', literally 'Anointed One', which would usually indicate a king. It's a title, but was quickly assumed to be a personal name by people outside the Jewish milieu.

You haven't really mentioned the Bible as a source of information. How come?

I'll explain more about the Bible, its nature, and what I believe about it in the next section specifically on belief, but for now I'll explain why I haven't really quoted from it in this 'history' section.

When trying to do historical research into early Christianity, using the Bible as a source can be problematic. Firstly because it's naturally biased. The books of the New Testament were written by believers for believers, which means that as historical documents they have to be treated with care. These books weren't written as history. They weren't really about simply chronicling events. The events they do record are coloured by the beliefs that go with them. Those early followers of Christ were concerned with spreading what they understood as the good news about Jesus, and recording the communities' stories for their own remembrance and use in worship. The thing is, nobody apart from Christ-followers themselves thought Christianity as a movement was worth writing about until a fair bit later, because it was so small and involved people of such low social status. All of which means it's hard to find secondary evidence for things recorded about the very earliest days of Christianity.

Secondly, the New Testament was compiled by the winners. You know how they say that history is written by the winning side? Well, the same thing is true of the Bible. In the earliest days of Christianity, people who followed Jesus came from all kinds of backgrounds and believed all kinds of different details about who Jesus was. Lots of different things were written down. But it was a church council who decided what should actually 'count' as being proper to include in the Bible. It meant they could ignore all the stuff written by other Christ-followers that they didn't necessarily agree with. For example, when the writer of the letter to Timothy asserts that 'I permit no woman to teach or to have authority over men; she is to keep silent', you can be certain that there were women and communities doing the exact opposite. The problem is that their voices have been silenced. Although the presence of four separate Gospels rather than one harmonised version speaks to a concern for diversity in the early Church, there is still a sneaking question. If one set of voices were almost certainly silenced, what else might have been excluded over the centuries?

You said Christianity was low status, but didn't the whole of Europe become Christian? What happened?

There was a profound shift. In the early days of Christianity, the Christ-followers were generally of low social status and there weren't that many of them. The hard-line Jews found them infuriating because they were perverting how they understood their Jewish faith. The Romans saw them as a nuisance because of their refusal to behave as all Romans did, making the appropriate sacrifices to the gods and the Emperor. They made a fuss, got in the way, and their refusal to acknowledge the Roman gods could be viewed as refusal to bow to Roman rule, at the worst, could even be seen as active sedition. Over time, the Romans either regarded them as a nuisance that they could put up with or as a nuisance that needed to be eradicated.

That's where all that about Christians being thrown to lions comes from?

Yes. The differences in opinion meant there were some quiet periods when Christ-followers could just get on with their lives. But there were also terrifying periods of out and out persecution, with Christ-followers being arrested, imprisoned, tortured and killed. How bad things were tended to depend on the attitudes of individual communities. Christianity was illegal, so if the will was there in the local community, which is to say, the local Roman governor was in agreement, you could punish all the Christ-followers you wanted. Some governors tried to check out how the emperor felt, as we can see in a letter from Pliny the Younger to Emperor Trajan dating from around 112 CE which asks what he should do about the local Christ-niks, but in general the governors just made their own decisions on an ad hoc basis.

That said, some emperors did take an active hand. Emperor Nero (who reigned 54–68 CE) is recorded by the Roman historian Tacitus as singling out Christ-niks to blame for the great fire in Rome in 64 CE. Emperor Domitian (81–96 CE) is said to have instituted some heavy persecution of Christ-followers toward the end of shis reign. But some of the worst and most widespread persecutions came along with the accession of the Emperor Decius (249–251 CE). In January of 250 CE he published an edict demanding that all citizens were to sacrifice to the emperor in the presence of a Roman official and to obtain a certificate to prove they had done it. Any who didn't were arrested and executed. This time the persecution was organised and universal, and over the course of a year took a terrible toll on the Empire's Christian communities. Over the period of the next few emperors (Valerian, Diocletian, Galerius) punishment of Christians continued, with a refusal to sacrifice to the Roman gods sometimes earning exile, reduction in rank or fines, and sometimes death. The brutality reached its peak in the rule of Diocletian, in the form of the 'Great Persecution', during which nearly half of all martyrdoms in the early Church period occurred.

So how did Christianity move from all that to Christians ruling Europe?

Interestingly, public opinion during the government-organised persecutions was on the side of the Christ-followers, who were admired for their courage. So when Constantius took the throne in 293 CE he was already not too keen on the idea of continuing practices that were so against the feelings of the populace. As a result, the punishments slowed down markedly. They stopped entirely in 306 CE with the accession of his son Constantine, who actually really liked Christianity. The only problem was that the Empire was in a state of civil war, as Constantine battled the three other emperors who had been ruling the Roman Empire. So it took a while before Constantine's promotion of the Christian religion from persecuted to favoured was spread throughout the Empire. The 'Edict of Milan' in 313 CE legalised Christianity, putting a halt to persecution once and for all. Constantine was involved enough in Christianity to convene councils to decide church doctrine and sit in on their meetings, but at this stage Christianity was still just one religion among many.

The next big step was when Christianity was made the state religion of the Roman Empire, thanks to Emperor Theodosius I publishing the Edict of Thessalonica in 380 CE. From this point on, Roman life and Christianity were joined at the hip, and Church and State became very much one and the same. The difference was that even when the Roman Empire collapsed, Christianity continued.

But it has to be said, Europe alone is only a fragment of the whole picture of early Christianity.

I thought Christianity was a European thing. That's why there were all those missionaries later on, right?

Nope. That is to say, yes there were missionaries. We'll talk more about them later. But remember, Christianity began in the Middle East, and it didn't just move west, it moved east and south as well. By the fifth century, Syria, Asia Minor, Georgia, Armenia, North Africa and Ethiopia had all developed as important Christian strongholds. In fact, Christianity spread even further east, through Persia (modern-day Iran and Iraq), as far east as China, Mongolia and even Japan. The ancient Christian communities in these places all developed their own particular shades of Christianity. They might worship in different languages, believe subtly different things or have different relationships with secular power, but they were all recognisably Christian and all belonged to the one Church.

Schisms

You've been talking about this one Church. But aren't there lots of different types of Christianity?

Yes. New interpretations of Christianity emerge throughout the Church's history. Some ideas were adopted in some form or other, some were branded heretical and crushed out of existence, and some resulted in large-scale splits, creating whole new denominations – denomination being the name we give the different flavours of Christianity.

'Heretical'?

It means people who hold beliefs that conflict with official doctrine. They are often regarded as dangerous, in that they might mislead and corrupt other members of their belief system. I say 'belief system' because the concept of heresy is common to all faith systems and not just Christianity.

So what's generally behind these splits?

Most disagreements centre on one of three things.

First, on what constitutes holy Scripture and how it should be understood and used; second, on formal statements of belief – creeds – and what they contain; and third, on church structure, for example, who should hold office and authority in the Church, what ministry looks like and so on.

The first two major new ideas that emerged in Christianity ended up being denounced and crushed. The first was Gnosticism, which emerged around the end of the first century CE. There were numerous particular schools of thought that could be grouped under the broad term 'Gnostics', but they have in common a rejection of the Hebrew Scriptures, which were held to refer not to the real God, but to an evil 'demiurge', who created the flawed universe. In this thinking, the real God revealed by Jesus has nothing to do with the Creator God of the Jews. This was fought tooth and nail by other Christians, and the battle was concluded with the fundamental rejection of Gnosticism. The Jewish Scriptures were affirmed as being the work of the one true God, and their place in the holy canon of Christianity was confirmed.

The second major new idea was that of Montanism, a movement following a man named Montanus, in Phrygia, in the mountains of modern Asia Minor. Montanism was also known as 'the New Prophecy', referring to new revelations that Montanus claimed to have had from the Holy Spirit. The Church was worried by this, not so much because of what was in the revelations, but because the whole process had happened outside the Church's authority. It felt dangerously chaotic, and after prolonged debate the Montanists were expelled from the Church. This conflict, about whether the random gift of prophecy or the order and authority of the Church were the more important, was to arise again and again throughout the history of Christianity.

But what about actual splits? Like, where there was one Church there were then two?

There have certainly been many splits in the Church. I won't talk about them all here, because that would take for ever, and we're thinking about the Church of England in particular. Instead, I'll follow the chain of schisms – splits in the Church – that ultimately led to the Church of England, and some of the splits that have happened within the Church of England itself since it began.

So where did the breaking start?

The first major split was between the Western Latin Church, which would later be called the Roman Catholic Church, and the Eastern Church, which would come to be called the Eastern Orthodox Church. The split became formalised in 1054, but had been on the cards from a long time before then.

What happened?

It was the result of a lot of different things. The Eastern and Western parts of the Church had been clashing for centuries, and not just on matters of belief, although they argued about those too. They were at loggerheads on the basis of linguistic and political differences as well.

There were the political differences. Politically, the late Roman Empire wasn't simply a single entity ruled by a single Emperor. It had been split up for administrative purposes during the reign of Diocletian, with four Emperors being chosen to govern different areas: a junior and a senior Emperor for the West, and a junior and a senior Emperor for the East. 'West' meant the Western Empire up to and including modern Bosnia and Herzegovina north of the Mediterranean Sea and the coastal regions of North Africa from what became Morocco to half way through modern Libya. 'East' meant everything east of that (primarily modern-day Greece, Turkey, Israel and Egypt) up to the edge of the

Empire. It didn't work terribly well, since as soon as he died, the junior emperors were immediately at each others' throats to decide who would *really* be in charge. Cue a major civil war. Even though Constantine managed to unify the Empire again by the end of his reign, it wasn't a lasting change. The division between East and West resumed on an on–off basis after his death, and was fixed after the death of Theodosius I, the last emperor to rule a united empire.

Constantine had made a new capital for himself, which initially he called New Rome, but everyone else called Constantinople (modern Istanbul) in his honour. It became adopted as the seat of the Eastern Roman Empire. The result of all this was that there was a marked split between East and West. Add to this the fall of the Western Roman Empire, as invasions from the Vandals, Visigoths and Ostrogoths took more and more territory in Western Europe, and the East became the only remaining part of the Roman Empire. The western side was ruled by various different Germanic tribes, albeit Christian Germanic tribes. Europe was split in two.

Then we have the linguistic differences. In the West, Christians spoke Latin. In the East, they mainly spoke Greek. The problem was that as time went on, people who spoke both languages became few and far between. Communication was a real issue.

And finally, there were theological differences. There were two major sticking points. First, about how the Church was organised, and who had authority over whom. After the Council of Chalcedon in 451 CE the Church was divided into five major regions ('sees'), each controlled by a patriarch. In the West was the see of Rome. In the East were the sees of Constantinople, Alexandria, Antioch and Jerusalem. The Patriarch of Rome (who took the affectionate term for 'father' *papa* – which became 'pope' – towards the end of the third century) thought he ought to be the go-to guy. The other patriarchs disagreed.

The second major theological difference was about a particular section of the 'Creed', the Church's formal statement of what Christians believe. This section includes statements about the Christian belief that God is a Trinity – one God who is Father, Son and Spirit. (More about this belief and what this all means in the section on belief.) The problem was that the Church Council at Constantinople in 381 CE had decided on the form of creed it wanted to keep. But then the Western Church, largely following the ideas of the Western theologian Augustine, inserted an extra clause into the statement without checking that was okay with everyone else. What had previously read '[the Spirit] proceeds from the Father' now read '[the Spirit] proceeds from the Father *and the Son*'. This is known as the *filioque* clause. Needless to say, it wasn't okay. If you ask most Christians these days, this *filioque* clause is what they'll point to as the reason for the split between the churches that became Eastern Orthodox and Roman Catholic.

In the end the two sides, divided by geography, language, politics and theology, simply drifted apart. The formal acts (each side excommunicating the other) only put the cap on something that had been true for ages. They just weren't the same entity any more.

What does 'Catholic' actually mean?

It comes from the Greek *katholikos* and means 'universal' or 'all-embracing'. It refers to the universal scope of the Church. Interestingly, the Church of England also refers to itself as a catholic Church (with a small c), indicating its inclusiveness and universality.

So that's the Roman Catholic Church. How do we get from that to the Church of England?

That took a few more centuries. The Roman Catholic Church was well established in Europe, and it had spread to the extremes of the Roman Empire while that still existed, and beyond in the years after the Empire had fallen. By the time the Eastern and Western Churches formally split, even the edges of Europe had become Christian, including Scandinavia and of course the islands that were to become Ireland and Great Britain. This was the time of Christendom, when Christianity and secular power were absolutely hand in hand. All monarchs were Christians (albeit of varying levels of spiritual belief and moral behaviour) and the Church grew in wealth and power. Bishops, and especially the Bishop of Rome, the head of the Roman Catholic Church, wielded immense levels of power, political as well as spiritual.

Of course, being as large and powerful an institution as it became, the Church was also prone to corruption and excess. Certain clergy weren't above lining their own pockets and the powerful church elite involved themselves directly with political matters, including who should be making war on whom, and who should be ruling what. Plenty of monarchs had good reason to be angry and frustrated with the power of the Church. The other effect of wielding such great power was a strong desire not to lose it. As before, various new ideas about God and how Christians should be and behave arose over time, but when these were rejected they were increasingly punished in exactly the same way as the Roman Empire had initially dealt with this rebellious new sect – with imprisonment, torture and death.

All this came together in a powerful cocktail at the beginning of the sixteenth century. The Roman Catholic Church had taken to selling 'indulgences', pieces of paper that guaranteed a certain number of years off their time in a section of the afterlife called 'purgatory', where people expected to serve a certain amount of time after death being punished for whatever sins they had committed in life. In Germany at this point, indulgences were being sold specifically to raise money to rebuild St Peter's Basilica in Rome and to support the Archbishop of Magdeburg in the manner to which he was accustomed. Theologically this was dubious to say the least. It was this, along with a number of other complaints and ideas, that caused a young monk named Martin Luther to nail a document listing his thoughts and complaints to the church door in Wittenberg, a university town in Saxony, asking for these various things to be debated. The year was 1517 and the document was his famous '95 Theses'.

The church leadership, with its heavy-handed approach to holding on to its power and authority, tried to crush this attempt to bring its actions into question. However, Luther's ideas had struck a chord and with the political support of the Elector of Saxony, his act of protest turned into a full and unexpected rebellion. This movement is known as the 'Reformation', and its leaders, most notably Martin Luther in Germany, Ulrich Zwingli in Switzerland and later John Calvin in France and Switzerland, were known as the 'Reformers'. However, the movement that resulted from their work is more widely known these days as 'Protestantism', since its followers 'protested' within and against the Roman Catholic Church of the time.

Protestantism? That's kind of the opposite of Roman Catholicism, right?

Not entirely. These days Protestants and Catholics are often drawn as being diametrically opposed, especially thanks to the Troubles in Northern Ireland, but the fact is that they have more in common than they have dividing them.

So what's the difference between Protestants and Catholics?

Interestingly, some of the things that were different back when Protestantism had only just arrived have actually been resolved now.

What were the issues back then?

Language. One of the major differences was that the Protestants wanted to worship in their own languages. Up to this point the language of Christianity in the West was Latin (in the East it was Greek), and all the services were conducted in Latin. Not much use if your language was German, or

French or English. People had routinely been attending
services with absolutely no idea what the priest was saying.

They also wanted all Christians to have access to
copies of the Bible and the chance to read it for themselves.
Unfortunately, the Bible too was only available in Latin, in
an edition known as the Vulgate Bible. There had been a few
translations at least of parts of the Bible into other languages
before the sixteenth century, but they were few and far
between. Also, in the Middle Ages the norm was for any
translations to be suppressed by the church leadership. As
now, knowledge was power. The Reformers wanted the Bible
to be translated into modern languages and freely distributed.

Simplification of thought and practice. There was also
a feeling that the Roman Catholic Church had become filled
with too many distractions, which meant the core of the
Church's message – the salvation brought by Jesus Christ –
had got lost. This was both in the form of physical stuff, in the
fact that by and large the Church was immensely wealthy,
and churches had more than their fair share of gold and silver,
jewels and velvet floating around. For the Reformers, this
didn't sit well with the Jesus we meet in the Gospels, who had
demanded the rich man sell all that he had and that everyone
should practise love towards those in need. What business had
the Church in being rich?

But this feeling that the Church was caught up in
distractions was also directed towards worship and belief.
Worship was complex: services were long and convoluted, not
to mention incomprehensible for your average man or woman
on the street. A Sunday service of Matins (morning prayer)
and Mass (Holy Communion) could last upwards of three
hours, and people would come and go throughout, chatter
among themselves and be generally boisterous. What was
more, worship didn't just involve addressing yourself to God.
Prayers were also offered to and through various saints and
especially the Virgin Mary. For the Reformers, all this got in
the way. They pushed for the Church to become simpler. No
more rich vestments and other trappings for the priests and

churches, a simplification of images and other art, stripping down worship services and getting rid of prayers to saints and the Virgin Mary.

Cutting out inequality. Finally, there was a move to lose at least some of the hierarchy of the Church. In the Roman Catholic Church at that time there was a strong sense of hierarchy that echoed the secular hierarchy that you saw in the governance of nations. The Pope was at the top, and power moved down in a pyramid structure through archbishops and bishops, priests, and then finally lay people. There was effectively a massive divide between the ordained members of the Church and the ordinary people.

This was shown most clearly in the case of Holy Communion. When a priest celebrated a service of Holy Communion as he did every Sunday, he did so hidden away behind a screen at the front of the church, and ate and drank the blessed bread and wine *in the place of* the congregation. The ordinary people gathered in the church just watched – they didn't share in the bread and wine at all. Instead, they were blessed by simply seeing the blessed bread raised at the moment it was blessed. Once a year at Easter they would actually eat some of the blessed bread (but none of the wine). In England this was referred to as 'taking one's rights'. The Reformers wanted to lose what they saw as inequality among God's people. They felt that everyone should be able to share in both the bread and wine as often as Holy Communion was celebrated. As for the hierarchical structure, all the Reformers wanted the Church to be free of the Pope's authority, but some wanted to lose the top-down hierarchy of the Church as a whole: pope, bishops, priests and all. As we shall see, this was by no means agreed by everyone who came under the banner of the Reformation.

So these things aren't issues any more?

Some of them aren't. These days the language issue has disappeared. The Bible has been translated into hundreds of different languages to be used by everyone, and both Roman Catholics and the Churches that sprang from the Reformation have at least some services in the vernacular. That said, the Roman Catholic Church does still celebrate the Mass in Latin as well as in local languages.

However, the issue of inequality between ordained clergy and lay people is still there to some extent. Although it's now the norm for congregations from Protestant traditions to share the bread and wine at all services of Holy Communion and to receive both bread and wine, in Roman Catholic churches it's still common for the congregation to only receive the bread.

So what are the differences between them now?

The major differences fall in the areas of appearances and belief. The Reformation wanted the physical appearances of their office-holders and churches to be stripped down and simplified. The Roman Catholic response was actually to beef up the richness of their churches and liturgy, their argument being that the beauty and complexity of the Church's appearance on earth is a pointer to those same qualities in God. This answering movement was called the Counter Reformation, and its effects can be seen today in Roman Catholic churches, and especially in the wealth of Roman Catholic art and music.

Similarly, the Reformers wanted to get back to the essentials of belief, and so stripped away what they saw as unnecessary distractions in spirituality and worship from the central truth of Christianity, namely Jesus, his life, death and resurrection. The Roman Catholics on the other hand made a concerted effort to retain the diversity in their spirituality. Saints and the Virgin Mary are still venerated today – something which Protestants find particularly hard to understand.

In terms of hierarchical structures, obviously the Roman Catholic Church didn't change at all. The Churches that came out of the Reformation vary in their structures, but one thing they have in common is that none of them look towards a single figure in the way that Roman Catholics look to the Pope.

It doesn't seem like they're that different at all. Why does everyone have this image of Catholics and Protestants being totally different and at each other's throats?

That has to do with the circumstances around the breaking away of the Protestant believers. You know how the split between the Eastern and Western Churches was pretty simple, in that it ended up being a formalising of a natural split based on geography, politics, culture and language? None of that was true in this case. It was horrendously messy. Protestant groups emerged all over Europe. Nations and settlements were split between those loyal to the old way and those wanting to follow this new way of thinking and worshipping. Worse, politics was involved wholesale from the beginning, and countries and regions began facing off with each other on the basis of whether their rulers were Roman Catholic or supporters of the Protestants. Wars followed, most notably the terrible Thirty Years War, one of the direct causes of which was the clash between Roman Catholics and Protestants.

As Protestantism began to be adopted by secular rulers it meant that they wielded the power to suppress supporters of Roman Catholicism. It wasn't long before Roman Catholics were burning Protestants at the stake, and Protestants were burning Roman Catholics. At the same time both Protestants and Roman Catholics felt free to kill followers of other breakaway groups such as the Anabaptists (of whom more below).

The suppression of the opposite group in secular states that identified as either Roman Catholics or Protestants continued well into the modern era. The bitterness of the divide between these two different 'flavours' of Christianity was huge, and is still deeply felt in some areas where the clashes were particularly heated. Ireland is a key example of a place where the division is especially rooted thanks to the political machinations that embedded the conflict.

You keep talking about 'Churches' that emerged out of the Reformation. There are different Protestant Churches?

Yes. They all identify as Protestant, but there are a number of different particular manifestations of Protestantism. Some of the differences are regional. Each region, now that the Pope's authority had been rejected, wanted to have their own national church. Some of the differences are in practice, often depending upon which of the reforming figures they follow. Lutheran (followers of Martin Luther's teachings), Calvinist (also simply called 'Reformed', followers of John Calvin's teachings) and Zwinglian (you get the idea) Churches all do things slightly differently.

Then you have the movements that were even more radical than the other reforming traditions, particularly Anabaptists. The Anabaptists rejected the idea of infant baptism, insisting that a baptism could only be real if it were the result of an adult decision to follow Christ. Anabaptist literally means 're-baptiser' because they practised full-immersion baptism of adults in rivers, despite those adults already having been baptised as babies. They weren't popular with either the Roman Catholics or other Protestants, and found themselves hunted down and killed as a result.

Basically there are a wide variety of Churches that might be grouped under the broad heading of 'Protestant', mainly in Northern Europe where Protestantism first emerged. France, Germany, England, Scotland, Ireland, Sweden, Norway, Denmark and Finland all have large Protestant populations.

And the Church of England was one of these Protestant Churches?

Ish. The Church of England is complicated. This needs a whole new section.

The Church of England

But the Church of England is Protestant, right?

No, not really, although it has Protestant elements. Let's start from the beginning. There had, of course, been a Christian church *in* England for centuries. Officially, ever since St Augustine of Canterbury launched his mission to the British mainland in 597. In fact, Christianity had been on the British mainland significantly before then. The first British martyr, for example, was St Alban, who was killed in the early third century. Celtic Christianity established strongholds on the mainland early, spreading from the north and west, from Ireland, Wales and Scotland, and slowly made its way south and east. The two types of Christianity, Roman Christianity spread by St Augustine, and Celtic Christianity, met in the middle, and had something of a formal showdown at the Synod of Whitby in 664. The outcome was a win for Roman Christianity, which became the default form of Christian faith from then onwards.

But you know how the Church *of* England first appeared?

It was Henry VIII, wasn't it? He wanted a divorce, so created a whole new church to do it?

Yep. But the part of the story that sometimes gets missed is that Henry VIII, before his marital issues, was a good Roman Catholic. In fact, that's where the title 'Defender of the Faith', still used by the royal family today and indeed printed on our coins, comes from. It was given to Henry VIII by the then Pope, Pope Leo X, as a reward for Henry writing the book *Assertio Septem Sacramentorum* (*In Defence of the Seven Sacraments*), which defended the sacramental nature of marriage and the supremacy of the Pope. Back then, Henry was very anti the Reformation, and the book underlined his opposition to Protestantism, and especially the teachings of Martin Luther. This was back in 1521.

Sacramental?

More on what 'sacramental' means in the section on belief. But to give a simplified overview, a 'sacrament' is an action or practice that communicates the grace and power of God in a specific and special way. One of the differences between Roman Catholics and Protestants is in what they regard as sacraments. Roman Catholics think there are seven: baptism, confirmation, matrimony, Holy Eucharist (Holy Communion), penance (also called confession), Holy Orders (ordination) and anointing of the sick (which most people are aware of from the Last Rites, the practice of anointing a person just before death). Protestants on the other hand vary in what they think constitutes a sacrament, but they pretty well all think there are less than seven. The usual position is that there are only two: Holy Communion and baptism, because they are the only two that actually appear in the Gospels. Some Lutherans add confession and absolution to this shortened list.

Hold on, did you just say Henry VIII wrote a book defending both marriage and the Pope?

Quite. 'Ironic' doesn't even begin to cover it.

If Henry was such a good Roman Catholic, where did the whole 'founding my own church' thing come from?

It was the result of a snowballing series of choices. Henry's first marriage, to Catherine of Aragon, only produced a girl, and Henry wanted sons. Plus, he had his eye on another nice English girl, Anne Boleyn. He wanted to quietly get rid of Catherine and move onto someone whom he thought was a better bet for a male heir.

The problem was that divorce wasn't a thing back then. When someone wanted to get rid of their spouse they needed to get the marriage 'annulled', that is, made as if it never happened. Usually the grounds for this would be if the marriage was never consummated, that is, the couple never had sex. Powerful men had been getting rid of their wives like this for a good long time. So Henry asked the Pope if he could get his marriage to Catherine annulled. And much to his horror, the Pope refused.

Why?

Politics, mainly. Catherine of Aragon was well connected. Well connected to the extent that her nephew was Charles V, the Holy Roman Emperor (meaning that he controlled vast swathes of Europe). The Pope, who by this time was Pope Clement VII, wanted Charles on his side, partly because at this point Protestantism was on the rise and secular regions were beginning to declare themselves for the Reformers and he wanted all the supporters of Roman Catholicism he could find; partly because Charles was putting him under pressure. And by 'pressure' I mean strongly intimating that his soldiers would be more than happy to sack Rome if Clement did something he wasn't happy with. So faced with Henry's desire to cast off a royal princess of Spain like so much used laundry, the Pope said no.

And Henry didn't take that well.

To say the least. He wanted the marriage annulled, and the Pope wouldn't do it. Logically, or what passes for logic if you're a person of Henry's astonishing self-belief, the next step was to take the ball out of the Pope's court. He had been having issues with papal authority for some time, feeling himself limited politically and economically (much as some feel towards the EU today). This seemed to be the answer to all his problems. He asserted that the Pope no longer had

jurisdiction over the Church in England, and named himself as
the English Church's supreme head.

So he created a Protestant Church of England?

Sorry, still no. Henry wasn't a Protestant. He didn't like
Protestants, and had had a good few of the English Reformers
burned. But when the legal process for breaking away from
Rome began in 1534, Henry was helped through it by two men
who were very much involved in the Protestant Reformation.
These were the two Thomases: Thomas Cromwell, the royal
minister, and Thomas Cranmer, Archbishop of Canterbury.
It was their work which discreetly pushed the English
Reformation forward. Laws were passed: making all clergy
take an oath of loyalty to the crown, instituting reforms in
religious practice, and even dissolving religious communities of
monks, nuns and friars, claiming their wealth and land for the
King.

If the Church in England was being changed like that, surely Henry knew what he was doing?

Not really. Most of the work was done by Cromwell and
Cranmer not entirely with the King's knowledge, and Henry
himself had strange mood swings when it came to religious
matters. Despite the fact he had cut himself free from the
Pope, Henry's belief and practice were still largely Catholic.
And every so often he stuck his oar in. As a result, the Church
of England was a strange mixture of Protestant bits added to a
Roman Catholic base, with the Protestant bits often watered
down when Henry had a change of heart a few years later.

For example, Henry's agents had had one of the geniuses
of the English Reformation, William Tyndale, arrested and
executed (strangled at the stake, and his body then burned)
while Tyndale was exiled in Antwerp. Tyndale had made his
life's work the translation into English of the New Testament
and the first five books of the Old Testament, a work of vital

importance for those English Reformers who wanted to read and spread the Bible in the common language of the nation. Henry didn't like that, so he had Tyndale killed for his efforts. But then, just a year after Tyndale's martyrdom, the King, at Cromwell's suggestion, authorised Tyndale's own translation of the New Testament for use in every parish in England. Then seven years later he tried to ban certain segments of the population (i.e. the lower classes) from reading it.

Thomas Cromwell discovered the danger of the King's changes of direction pretty early on, when the King had him executed for furthering the Reformation and (probably more importantly in the King's eyes) for failing to find Henry a decent wife who could produce male heirs. In particular, for only managing to find him Anne of Cleves, who wasn't Henry's favourite bride ever. The moral of the story was: when it came to Henry VIII and religion you never knew what he was going to do next.

So what exactly happened to the Church of England on Henry's watch?

He gutted it, pretty well. He executed a large number of priests for refusing to take the oath of loyalty and abandon the Pope. He closed every single monastery, convent and friary in England and Wales, communities which had been a vital part of the English landscape for centuries. He brought in changes to worship and religious practice that he later tried to reverse or at least water down. When he died, the Church was a confused mess, which needed some serious rebuilding. All of which proved fertile ground for Henry's immediate successor, his son Edward VI. Edward had been raised Protestant and had Cranmer as his guide and advisor. He and his advisors were ready to take Protestantism in England forward without Henry's strange vacillating between Catholic and Protestant sensibilities.

So Henry VIII created the Church of England, but it was Edward VI who made it Protestant?

Yes, but that's not the end of the story by a long way. Edward did indeed make the Church of England part of the Protestant Reformation. He authorised a new prayer book, *The Book of Common Prayer*, with editions published in 1549 and 1552, largely written by Cranmer. And he authorised the use of English translations of the Bible. But unfortunately for the English Reformation, he died very young.

So what?

So the person who followed him onto the throne of England was Mary I, Catherine of Aragon's (remember her?) daughter, Edward's elder half-sister. Mary was a devout Roman Catholic and soon after her accession to the throne was married to the King of Spain. She didn't want a Protestant Church of England. For her, Protestants were heretics. As soon as she took the throne she began trying to reverse all the changes that had been made in Edward's reign. Nor was she shy about getting rid of those in her way. Mary has gone down in history as 'Bloody Mary' for the number of English Protestants she burned at the stake, including the unfortunate Cranmer.

She made the Church of England Catholic again?

Yes.

This is just confusing.

Imagine how the ordinary citizens of Britain felt. Being burned at the stake became an everyday hazard.

But the Church of England isn't Catholic!

No. That's thanks to the monarch who came after Mary I, the much celebrated Elizabeth I.

So what did Elizabeth I do?

She, with her very able advisors, created the 'Elizabethan Settlement' in 1559, an arrangement in two parts, which brought together elements of both Catholic and Protestant beliefs to form a single Church. This Church was moderately reformed in its beliefs, but still held on to Catholic tradition and continuity. English theologians of this period saw the Church of England as engaging in a reformation that brought it closer to the very roots of Christian belief and worship. It wasn't about creating new things, it was about getting back to the way things should be. The other change was that the Church was 'established', meaning that each new monarch automatically becomes Supreme Head of the Church of England when they take the throne.

So the Church of England is both Catholic and Protestant?

That's about it. That said, the really important thing to remember is that the Church of England doesn't regard itself as having come into existence out of nothing back in 1534 when Henry VIII cut ties with Rome. Instead, it's the successor of that same church that had been in England ever since those first martyrs in the third century. It held on to many of its worship practices, albeit now reformed, its church law, its parish structure, its cathedrals and its bishops.

But don't Catholics and Protestants believe different things about all kinds of stuff?

They do indeed. But the biggest differences between Catholics and Protestants were ironed out through the '39 Articles of Religion', which stated the broad beliefs that the Church of England should hold on a variety of hot topics. It

took 30 years of discussion and editing for these articles to
be finalised, and their number rose and fell during this period,
but their final form as 39 statements was finally determined in
1571.

Vicars make an oath declaring their assent to these
Articles when they are ordained. However, in practice there
have always been vicars who don't sign up to one or more of
the Articles.

*How was it possible for the Church of England to be Catholic and
Protestant? Didn't the sides clash?*

Generally the extremes of belief in the Church of England
rub along all right, thanks to the Elizabethan idea of
'comprehension', that is, members of the Church of England
were and are free to place their own private interpretations on
what goes on in liturgy as long as no one makes a public fuss
about it. It means that Anglican doctrine can be on the fuzzy
side, as everyone can put their own spin on matters of belief.

However, this inclusive understanding of matters of
belief doesn't always work. From time to time Catholic
and Protestant elements in the Church of England clash,
sometimes to terrible effect. With the Elizabethan Settlement
the Church of England included within itself supporters of
quite distinct ways of understanding and worshipping God. On
the one side you had those of a more Catholic persuasion, who
liked rich and complex services, churches and clerical dress,
who continued to venerate the saints and the Virgin Mary.
And on the other side you had the radical Protestants, who
wanted simple and sober worship, who loathed everything that
seemed to be connected with the Roman Catholic Church and
denounced such things as 'popery'. This latter group were also
known as Puritans.

These two elements within the Church were very
delicately balanced, and it didn't take much to push things out
of alignment and make trouble. Things became the worse they
had ever been for the newly fledged Church of England during
the reign of Charles I. He and his Archbishop of Canterbury,

William Laud, tried to push the Church of England much further towards the Catholic side. It was only one of many errors from Charles I, but it had major repercussions for the Church of England. The sum total of Charles's actions of course led to the horrific English Civil War.

In the aftermath of the war, in which people had aligned themselves along Catholic and Protestant lines as much as anything else – the supporters of the King being more Catholic, with the roundheads being more Protestant – the Church of England was gutted more seriously than Henry VIII had ever managed. Archbishop Laud was beheaded. The King, Charles I, the Supreme Governor of the Church of England, lost his head soon afterwards at the hands of the Puritan Oliver Cromwell. The government that followed, a Commonwealth under the control of Cromwell as Lord Protector, directed the Church to get rid of its bishops, its Prayer Book and its habits of worshipping. He and fellow Puritans wanted to purge any sign of 'popery' from churches, and sadly for us now, that included much of the ancient art and statuary that had adorned churches since medieval times. A common sight in pretty well every church that has been around since before the 1640s are the empty niches where statues of saints would have stood, or, more poignantly, just the bodies of those saints, their heads having been smashed apart. Places like the Lady Chapel at Ely Cathedral really bring it home: walls covered with beautiful painting scoured, bas relief images defaced, statue niches empty, stained glass smashed.

Basically, the Church of England was all but abolished.

The Restoration, Charles II's return to the throne in 1660, restored the Church of England as much as it did the monarchy. The fragile balance was back. However, the upheaval of the preceding 20 years wasn't easily forgotten, and there was serious distrust between the more Catholic and more Protestant elements. That distrust still hangs around today.

The present

'Church traditions' in the Church of England

You spoke before about 'church traditions'. What's all that about?

A person's 'tradition' or 'churchmanship' is a way of describing where they are on the Catholic–Protestant spectrum that makes up the broad membership of the Church of England. So someone with a 'high' tradition tends more towards the Catholic end of that spectrum. They might enjoy the use of candles, incense (used to symbolise prayers ascending to God, and to recognise the various foci of worship such as the altar and the Gospels) and rich clerical vestments in churches, or find the celebration of Holy Communion particularly special and important, or find spiritual sustenance in a detailed, solemn liturgy. They may find it appropriate to pray for the dead or to venerate the Virgin Mary and other saints. And when I say 'enjoy', I really mean 'find spiritually helpful and nourishing'. Everyone finds themselves spiritually moved and fed by different things. I personally would say that none of these are 'right' or 'wrong', just different.

Liturgy?

Liturgy is our term for the content of worship, whether public services or more private occasions. It covers the words spoken, the prayers said, the movement that occurs during the service, the hymns sung, and basically everything that makes up an act of worship.

And a 'low' tradition?

Someone with a low tradition would tend more towards the Protestant end of the spectrum. They might like a special emphasis on preaching and the use and teaching of the Bible in services, or a more informal style of communal worship, or a simpler style of church appearance and clerical dress.

As a vicar, do you bring your own personal tradition to the churches you work in?

A little. When we apply for a new post, we'll pay attention to what the parish says about its own tradition. If the parish is clearly right at the high end of the spectrum and your preferred style of worship is at the low end, you would be unlikely to go for that post, simply because either you or the congregations in that parish would find the worship spiritually unsatisfying. So generally you'll choose a parish that worships in a way you find spiritually helpful.

That said, in training we're encouraged to get some experience of serving in parishes that belong to traditions different from our own. It's good to realise just how broad this Church of ours is, and to recognise the value of different styles of worship. All of which means we are generally able to work in a parish that doesn't practice the kind of worship with which we're most comfortable.

It's also possible to introduce some new practices gently and gradually into a parish to see if people like them and find them spiritually useful. You don't have to stick to what's always been done indefinitely. That said, change is always tough, no matter how gentle you may be.

What you really can't do, and problems ensue when you ignore this fact, is try to remake a parish into your image wholesale. Apart from that kind of thing ruining the trust relationship with the parish, the Parochial Church Council has to pass all the changes you might want to make to worship, from what vestments you wear to the prayers you use. You would have a tremendous fight on your hands if you tried to force them in a direction they didn't like. Plus it would just be thoroughly disrespectful.

Governing the Church of England

Should Church and State be separate?

They're not at the moment. The Church of England is an established Church, which means it's bound up with the State. Church law is included in the law of the land, the sitting

Prime Minister has a voice in the selection of the Archbishop
of Canterbury, and the head of the state Government, the
Queen, is also head of the Church.

There are some great things about being established. I
think the most important thing is that it makes the Church of
England responsible for the spiritual welfare of the nation. On
a local level, what that means is that a vicar doesn't just look
out for the people who come to church on a Sunday. They are
there to serve every single person who lives within the parish
boundaries, whether or not they believe in God or come to
church. If someone dies within the parish, they are *bound by
law* to conduct that person's funeral if that's what the deceased
and/or their family want. They are *bound by law* to conduct
the wedding or the baptism of a person living in the parish if
that's something the person wants. It means the Church has to
be open to everyone, and it's a good counterweight against the
inclination to be closed and self-serving.

On the other hand, it does tie the Church to particular
(very expensive to maintain) buildings, and makes it rather
harder to make changes in church law and policy, since at
the moment they also have to be passed by Parliament. The
American concept of the need to divide Church and State
isn't really applicable in the UK situation. Religious tolerance is
the word of the day, and neither Church nor State finds itself
limited or compromised by an association with the other.

Now if the State began to try to make changes to the
Church, which it conceivably might try to do given the
Church's recent debates over same-sex partnerships and
women bishops, that might be more of a problem. At the
moment, though, I think the established Church works fine,
and there's no need for Church and State to be separated.

You've mentioned a 'synod' a few times. What's that?

'Synod' is the name for a decision-making meeting within
the Church. There are basically three levels of synod. The
first includes all clergy and elected representatives from
congregations in a deanery, and is called, as you might expect,

a deanery synod. The next level has slightly more power, and involves the bishops, elected clergy (not all of them automatically, as at deanery level) and lay people from within a diocese, making it a diocesan synod. The highest level is the General Synod, which as with the diocesan synod is divided into three sections, named 'houses'. These are:

- The House of Bishops
  - 44 diocesan bishops
  - 8 suffragan bishops, elected by all suffragan bishops
- The House of Clergy
  - 182 clergy elected from diocesan synod representatives
  - 6 elected university representatives
  - 6 deans of cathedrals
  - Either the Dean of Guernsey or the Dean of Jersey
  - 1 Chaplain each from the RAF, Royal Navy and Army
  - the Chaplain-General of Prisons
  - 2 members of religious communities (i.e. monks and nuns)
- The House of Laity
  - 250 elected lay representatives from diocesan synods
  - the Dean of the Arches
  - the Vicars-General of both Canterbury and York
  - the 3 Church Estate Commissioners
  - the Chair of the Central Board of Finance
  - the Chair of the Church of England Pensions Board
  - Members of the Archbishops' Council who are also members of the Church of England.

Lots of new terms there. 'Dean of the Arches'?

The Dean of the Arches is the judge who sits on the Archbishop of Canterbury's ecclesiastical court, often called the Arches Court.

Ecclesiastical?

As in 'belonging to the Church'. It comes from the Greek for a gathering – an ekklesia – and came to be used exclusively for Christian gatherings, which is to say, the Church.

There are church courts?

Yes. Although these days they only deal with disciplinary proceedings for clergy and issues around church property.

And this is an actual judge?

Yes. He or she (he at the moment, although his predecessor was a woman) is a qualified judge and senior lawyer.

'Vicars-General' in the House of Laity? I thought a vicar was definitely ordained?

Not in this case. The Vicars-General are neither vicars nor generals, but senior ecclesiastical lawyers. Their courts confirm the formal election of a diocesan bishop, but their role isn't just ceremonial. Mostly they are occupied with the general legal work of the Church at national level.

And 'Church Estate Commissioners'?

The Church Commissioners are the body who manage the central assets of the Church of England, and are responsible for things like clergy pay and pensions. The Church Estate Commissioners are the three members of the Church Commissioners elected to represent the whole at General Synod. The second member is an MP, and reports back to Parliament on the business of the Commissioners.

What's the 'Archbishops' Council', and who's on it?

The Archbishops' Council is the central executive body of the Church of England, and is reported to by the various church committees and boards. It is made up of:

- the Archbishop of Canterbury
- the Archbishop of York
- the Prolocutors of the Convocations of Canterbury and York
- the Chair and Vice-Chair of the House of Laity of the General Synod
- 2 bishops elected by the House of Bishops of the General Synod
- 2 clergy elected by the House of Clergy of the General Synod
- 2 lay people elected by the House of Laity
- 1 of the Church Estates Commissioners
- pp to 6 other people jointly appointed by the 2 Archbishops, with the consent of the General Synod.

'Prolocutors'?

These are the elected joint chairs of the House of Clergy, elected from among its members.

'Convocations'?

There are two convocations, one for the province of Canterbury, and the other for the province of York. A convocation consists of the province's archbishop, along with bishops (all diocesan bishops and a few elected suffragan/area bishops) forming an 'upper house' and other clergy (elected at diocesan level) forming a 'lower house'.

Do all vicars know all this stuff?

It may just be me (although I hope it isn't!) but I've certainly had to look a lot of this information up. Knowing all the ins and outs of the various councils and representatives isn't something taught at theological college, and isn't really necessary for the day-to-day running of a parish.

So what does the General Synod do?

It's the main decision-making body of the gathered Church of England, so it does a number of important things.

- It passes legislation. This can be done in two ways. Firstly by 'measures', which are then passed on to Parliament to approve (or not), and if passed become part of the law of the land. Measures usually relate to the government of the Church. Secondly, it can pass legislation by means of 'canons', which determine doctrine (that is, what the Church believes) and forms of worship.
- It regulates relations with other Christian denominations and can make provisions for matters relating to worship and doctrine.
- It determines the use of liturgy by approving, amending, continuing or discontinuing various forms of liturgies.
- It considers any other matters of religious or public interest.
- And finally it approves (or rejects) the central church budget each year.

Can people really claim 'sanctuary'? If so, what would you have to do?

Not any more, at least not in law. From the reign of Ethelbert in 600 CE it was possible to legally avoid arrest by claiming sanctuary in a church. However, this law was abolished in 1623.

That said, there is still a powerful idea common to all religions that places of worship should be places of peace and safety. Even if it's not backed up in law, people still take shelter in religious buildings to this day.

Women in the Church of England

So women as priests in the Church of England ... When did that happen?

It was a long time coming. Around the end of the nineteenth century, when women were beginning to push for their rights in all kinds of different arenas, they were also pushing for the opportunity to serve as ordained members of the Church. This manifested as the Deaconess Movement, with women campaigning to be ordained as deaconesses. The first woman to be licensed as a deaconess in the Church of England was Elizabeth Ferard, in July 1862. She and her fellow deaconesses lived in residential communities (like nuns), but under the guidance of Isabella Gilmore, ordained deaconess in 1887, their ministry expanded to be parish-based, and the practice of ordaining deaconesses spread throughout the country.

This was a step forward, but there was still a long way to go. Maude Royden, a campaigner for women's suffrage, also spoke up in urging the Church to open ministry to women. In 1929 Royden founded the Society for the Ministry of Women. Despite the work of Royden and others, the Church didn't really give the matter of women's ordination further thought until the 1960s. In 1975 the General Synod declared that 'there are no fundamental objections to the ordination of women to the priesthood'. Nobody did anything about it, though, and campaigning continued.

In 1987 there was the first progress for a long while, when women were ordained as permanent deacons. Then in 1992 the General Synod agreed that women would be ordained as priests. The first women were ordained as priests in March 1994, in Bristol.

What was it like for the first women priests?

Obviously I can't speak from experience, but it was tough.
Some parishes refused to accept the idea of women's ministry
at all. Synod passed Resolutions A and B, which offered
parishes the option of refusing women's ministry. These are
still operational today. In addition, an Act of Synod was passed
in 1993, creating 'flying bishops' for those who wouldn't accept
the ministry of bishops who ministered alongside ordained
women.

Aside from these official opt-outs, even in parishes
that nominally accepted women's ministry there are stories
of rejection and even harassment. This ranged from the
reasonably mild, such as parishioners not accepting the bread
and wine when they were blessed by a female priest, to the
outright aggressive, such as women priests being spat at.
Sadly, such activity came from ordained men as well as lay
men and women. I can't imagine how awful it must be to be
abused in such way by a brother priest.

*What is it like for women in the Church of England now? Are
they completely welcomed?*

No, not completely. Some dioceses are particularly
unwelcoming to women priests, often due to the presence
of a diocesan bishop who rejects women's ministry. As I
said above, Resolutions A and B are still alive and well in the
Church of England, so some parishes, even in dioceses largely
accepting of women's ministry, remain off limits for women
priests. Even in parishes that have a female vicar, there are
often still pockets of opposition, which can make life difficult.
I have been lucky so far in that I've felt wholly welcomed
wherever I've gone, but I'm not naive enough to think that will
be the case throughout my future ministry. It has to be said,
though, the number of parishes opposed to women's ministry
has declined markedly in the years since women were first
ordained priests.

Are there times when people prefer a male vicar to a female vicar?

It's not very common, but it does happen. In my experience
in a very welcoming parish, there have been a number of
occasions when people have particularly asked for a male
priest. This happens most often when taking funerals, but I
know some people won't come to Holy Communion services
if they know a woman will be taking the service. For some
people it's a matter of faith and conscience, for others it's just
personal taste. Often, I suspect, it's a combination of the two.

However, although there are occasions when people
prefer male to female ministry, there are occasions when the
reverse is also true. I've experienced a number of cases in my
time as an ordained minister when an individual or family has
specifically requested female ministry. For me this has been in
respect to two particular types of ministry: funeral ministry
and home visits.

*You said in the past women priests have attracted harassment
from fellow clergy. Does that still happen?*

Only extremely rarely, I think. There are still cases of rudeness
and bullying: women vicars blanked at diocesan gatherings, for
example, but nothing like the antipathy that was around when
women first began to be ordained.

What's going on about women bishops?

It's all a bit of a mess at the moment. Right now women can't
be bishops in the Church of England. They can and are in
other parts of the Anglican Communion including Wales,
Ireland, the USA, Canada and New Zealand. The Church is
trying to pass legislation to allow women to be bishops in the
Church of England, but is having trouble because no one can
agree about how best to accommodate those members of the
Church who do not accept women's ministry.

Those who can't accept women's ministry want it in law
that they will still be able to have male priests ordained by a

bishop who doesn't also ordain female priests, and that they won't have to accept the oversight and leadership of a female bishop. Those in favour of women bishops want to make sure that the legislation doesn't create two tiers of bishops, one for men, and one for women which allows women's ministry to be limited. Thus far, no one's been able to suggest a form of words that satisfies all these requirements. The most significant recent development was the November 2012 vote by General Synod, which blocked the proposal for the creation of female bishops. In response to this, the legislation was redrafted and there was a first vote on this newly drafted legislation in July 2013. This was passed to go through to the next stage, but it's only the beginning of a process that will last a couple of years. It'll be July or August 2015 before the final decision will be made on this new draft.

The majority of church members and dioceses say they want women bishops. We just can't decide how to make that happen and keep everyone happy.

Why do you think people don't agree with women's ministry?

There are two main arguments that are generally made by those who don't accept female ministry, each coming from the opposite end of the spectrum of church tradition.

Firstly, the argument that often comes from those from a High Church tradition is around the fact of Jesus' maleness, and the fact that his 12 disciples were men. When priests lead services of Holy Communion and bless the bread and wine, they are participating in what Jesus did at the Last Supper. So, the argument goes, a woman can't act in the place of and in participation with Christ, because he was a man. In this high tradition, ordination is held to make a change in a person's actual being. An argument springs from this understanding, with people suggesting that ordination doesn't work in women as it does in men, because women weren't among Jesus' 12 disciples. This argument can be boiled down to the idea that ordination doesn't *work* for women.

Secondly, the argument that often comes from those of a lower church tradition is based upon the concept of male 'headship'. This is the idea that only men can and should hold positions of leadership, whether in public or in family life. It's been a common belief throughout history in many societies and belief systems, but also appears in the Bible, most particularly in a number of Paul's letters to early church communities. The idea in a Christian context is based on a concept of inherent hierarchy. Christ is the head of the Church and men are the heads of their families.

One of the readings that's most commonly quoted is from Paul's first letter to the Corinthians (1 Corinthians 11:3). He says, 'But I want you to understand that Christ is the head of every man, and the husband is the head of his wife, and God is the head of Christ.' A similar reading can be found in the first letter to Timothy (1 Timothy 2:12), where the author says, 'I permit no woman to teach or have authority over a man; she is to keep silent.'

Working from this starting point, the argument is simple. Only men can hold positions of authority over other men. Women cannot. The end.

You don't agree.

No. But then I'm an ordained woman. It would be odd if I did agree, wouldn't it?

What do you think, then?

With regard to the first argument, I think that just because something wasn't done for hundreds of years, that doesn't mean it won't work. It just means it hasn't been done. In his lifetime, Jesus didn't ordain priests. The office of 'priest' as we know it doesn't make an appearance in the New Testament. The closest we get are 'presbyters' in some of the later letters, a word which can best be translated as 'elders'. Saying that

Jesus didn't ordain women as priests is to say nothing at all. Jesus didn't ordain *anyone* as priests.

Nor do I think there is much value in the argument that Jesus didn't have women disciples, because he *did* have women disciples. Several women are mentioned by name in the Gospels as people who followed Jesus around the country, tended to his needs and listened to his teaching. If that's not a disciple, what is? Plus, Jesus chose to reveal his rising from the dead to a woman, Mary Magdalene, who was then trusted to spread the news to the other disciples. This to my mind, and indeed she's named as this in the Orthodox tradition, makes her the first apostle. Then of course, there's the fact that there were several important women among the earliest church communities: important enough for Paul to mention them by name in his letters. There is one, Phoebe, who is actually named as a deacon.

Finally, I don't think that one has to share Jesus' gender to participate in his work. Christian faith says that Jesus saved everybody, male and female, and that his spirit resides in us. If that's true, why should gender get in the way of another form of communion with Christ?

With regard to the second argument, I think this idea that women should be subject to men is a product of its time, and not a product of Jesus' teaching. Paul's general position was that Christians shouldn't rock the societal boat, since the world was probably going to end soon anyway. This meant there was no need to try to make major changes that some people would find difficult. So slaves shouldn't try to get themselves freed, for example. But these days we don't think slavery is a good idea. It's the same for the concept of women being socially inferior to men. It might have been the way things often were in the first century, but that doesn't make it the way things should be for ever.

The Church of England and other Christians

What are the main differences between Anglicanism and Roman Catholicism?

As we saw earlier, many of the things that had initially been points of conflict between Protestants and Catholics have now been resolved. Roman Catholics largely worship in the vernacular, in the local language of each church, and in the same way they're happy for the Bible to be translated into the vernacular. When you remember that Anglicanism has a fair slice of Catholicism in its make-up, you can see how they can be much closer than Catholics and fully Protestant Churches are now.

Modern scholarship into how the earliest form of the Church used to worship has brought the denominations together as everyone tries to be as true as they can be to the ancient traditions. Put a service sheet from a Roman Catholic service and a service sheet from a middle-of-the-road Anglican service side by side, and they would look almost no different from one another. The higher end of the Anglican tradition in particular is so close to Roman Catholicism as to be nearly indistinguishable, and in many cases is more 'Catholic' than Roman Catholics themselves!

The main difference is one of authority. Roman Catholics look to the Pope. Anglicans do not. The hierarchy is slightly different as well, in that Anglicans have bishops and archbishops, but not cardinals.

Which leads us to the second major difference: Anglicans are happy to recognise Roman Catholic clergy as properly ordained ministers in the universal Church. Roman Catholics on the other hand refuse to recognise Anglican clergy, at least officially. According to a papal proclamation from Pope Leo XIII in 1896 entitled *Apostolicae Curae*, Anglican orders are 'absolutely null and utterly void'. Which says it all, really. In practice, Roman Catholic clergy seem to be a little more generous, but the word from the top hasn't changed since 1896. An object demonstration of this difference is in who is allowed to receive Holy Communion in these two churches.

The Anglican Church is happy for Roman Catholics to
share in Holy Communion with them. The Roman Catholic
Church on the other hand forbids its members from receiving
Holy Communion at Anglican services, and refuses to allow
Anglican Christians to receive the bread and wine at its own
services.

The third difference is the ordination of women. Anglicans
ordain women to be priests (although not yet bishops – more
on that later), whereas Roman Catholics don't ordain women
at all. Now within the Church of England itself there are still
those who don't believe that women's ordination is valid, but the
Church as a whole has taken the step of ordaining women to
the priesthood, marking a major shift from the positions of both
the Roman Catholic and Orthodox traditions.

*But there are Christian churches in Great Britain that are neither
Roman Catholic nor belonging to the Church of England. Where
did they come from?*

Over the last three centuries or so there have been a number
of offshoots from the Church of England, and several
Churches that have grown up in the United States have made
their way to the UK. I won't go into them too much, because
this book is about the Church of England in particular, but
here's a brief summary of some of the Christian churches you
might find on a UK street.

Firstly, some of the mainstream Christian denominations:

Methodists. This was a movement that broke away from the
Church of England in the eighteenth century. It was triggered as
part of the 'Evangelical Revival' and the work of eminent figures
such as George Whitefield and John and Charles Wesley.
'Methodism' was characterised by fervent devotion, rigorous
self-discipline and outreach, especially through preaching.
Anglicanism's failure to accommodate and make use of the
energy behind this movement and keep its followers within
its fold was a profound loss. Methodists broke away from the
Church of England, stopped attending Anglican churches and

began building their own chapels. These days Anglicans and Methodists get on pretty well. We're what is known as 'in communion', meaning that we can worship together without issues, share buildings and services, and generally see each other as equals who just do things slightly differently.

Baptists. 'Baptist' is actually an umbrella term that includes a number of different denominations, all of whom worship in different ways and believe different things. One thing they have in common, though, is their belief that the only valid form of baptism is 'believers' baptism' – that is to say, the full-immersion baptism of adults, having made a mature decision to follow Christ. They all trace their roots to the English Separatists – those people on the far Protestant side of the Church of England who decided that the Church hadn't reformed enough and was still too Catholic. They broke away in the centuries following the Restoration of Charles II to the throne, and founded their own communities and churches. Baptist churches were one form of these.

Quakers. Like the Baptists, the Quakers emerged from the dissenting groups of the Church of England, and broke away in the mid-seventeenth century. Their founder was a man named George Fox who was convinced, through a religious experience, that it was possible to have a direct experience of Christ without the aid of ordained clergy. This conviction drove him to preach and spread this message far and wide, a practice which attracted particular persecution under the Quaker Act of 1662. Modern Quakers, properly called 'The Religious Society of Friends' are distinguished by their belief in the 'priesthood of all believers' (i.e. the idea that ordained clergy aren't necessary), their pacifism, and the silent worship practised by a number of the groups who include themselves among the Friends.

Presbyterians. Presbyterian churches are members of the Reformed (also called Calvinist) Protestant tradition, founded in sixteenth-century Zurich, Strasbourg and Geneva, and count Ulrich Zwingli, Martin Bucer and John Calvin among their most important leaders and theologians. 'Presbyterian' refers to a manner of church government, namely government through elected councils, called 'courts'. This means that Presbyterians don't have bishops. Rather each congregations has three types of office-holders: teaching elders (pastors), ruling elders and deacons. Pastors are ordained, and teach and lead worship. Ruling elders are elected by the congregation and lead and nurture the congregation. Deacons (sometimes ordained, but not always) take care of specific responsibilities such as care of buildings, finance and care of the needy. In the British Isles, the Presbyterian Church, like so many of the more Protestant denominations, broke away from the Church of England after the seventeenth-century Restoration.

United Reformed Church. The URC emerged in 1972, the result of the joining of the Presbyterian Church of England and the Congregational Church in England and Wales. It combines the Presbyterian method of governance through courts with the congregational emphasis on the local congregation, and its looser regional and national associations. Each congregation manages its affairs and arranges its services as it chooses, which means different congregations can do things quite differently to each other. On a wider scale, the congregations send representatives to regional synods, and there is a biennial General Assembly which brings elected representatives from the whole of the URC together and makes policy and strategy decisions for the denomination as a whole.

Pentecostals. Pentecostalism was actually originally an American renewal movement in the early twentieth century that has spread throughout the world, and has quite a strong presence in the UK now. Pentecostalists are distinguished by their belief in the importance of 'baptism in the Spirit' (receiving the power and gifts of the Holy Spirit following the laying on of hands of other believers) as giving direct personal experience of God. They also stress the importance of 'gifts of the Spirit' (speaking in tongues, prophecy, healing etc.) as spoken about in the New Testament, especially 1 Corinthians 12.

The Salvation Army. The Salvation Army had its beginnings in Methodism as a movement founded by a Methodist Minister, William Booth, and his wife Catherine in 1865. It was originally named the East London Christian Mission, with the aim of meeting the 'physical and spiritual needs' of the poor, hungry and destitute, an aim which continues today. Another distinguishing feature about the Salvation Army is that it has a quasi-military structure, including ranks and uniforms, with its ministers holding officer ranks and a General at the top. Its beliefs and practice are basically Methodist, but with a special emphasis on charitable works.

Secondly, a non-Trinitarian Church:

Unitarians. Whereas orthodox Christian denominations believe God to be a Trinity of Father, Son and Holy Spirit (more on this in the section on belief), Unitarians hold that the concept of the Trinity is contrary to monotheism and incorrect. For them, Jesus Christ was a great prophet and leader, but not God himself. They also hold broadly liberal positions on other elements of Christian doctrine, rejecting concepts such as original sin, predestination and the literal interpretation of the Bible.

And finally, some Churches which have their roots in Christianity, but are now distinctly on the fringes:

Christian Scientists. This was a movement that was developed in the late nineteenth century by an American named Mary Baker Eddy. Her book *Science and Health* is the Christian Scientists' central text alongside the Bible. Christian Scientists subscribe to the belief that the material world is an illusion, and the only reality is spiritual reality. This led to followers of Christian Science refusing all medical treatment

and vaccinations (since illness and disease are illusions that
need spiritual cures, not material ones), leading to several
deaths. However, since the 2000s Christian Science churches
have tried to present spiritual healing as a complement to
conventional medicine, and not a replacement.

Mormons. More properly called 'The Church of Jesus
Christ of Latter-Day Saints', Mormonism was founded by
Joseph Smith Jr. in New York in the 1820s, and broke away
from Protestantism. Their sacred texts include the Bible,
but also the *Book of Mormon*, written by Smith Jr. The *Book
of Mormon* is believed by members of the Latter-Day Saints
church to contain writings of ancient prophets who lived on
the American continent from 2200 BCE to 421 CE, and to be
an historical record of God's dealings with the inhabitants of
the continent. Early on, the Church taught polygamy, but this
was discontinued by the main body of the church by the end
of the nineteenth century. They are also strict about what
substances their adherents may put into their bodies, with all
kinds of drugs, including alcohol and caffeine, being prohibited.

Jehovah's Witnesses. Jehovah's Witnesses emerged from
the Bible Student Movement of 1870s New York, which
was seeking to 'return' to the true faith and was confidently
predicting the end of the world in 1925. Obviously this didn't
happen, and the Jehovah's Witnesses were one of several
groups who broke away from the main body of the movement
under the leadership of Joseph Franklin Rutherford. They
took the name 'Jehovah's Witnesses' in 1931 to distinguish
themselves. They use their own translation of the Bible – the
New World Translation of Holy Scriptures – and have as a
central tenet of their faith that we are currently living in the
end times, and look forward to the end of the world as we
know it in the near future. They refuse military service and
blood transfusions as part of their faith. They also do not
celebrate Christmas, Easter or birthdays. They are probably
best known for their door-to-door preaching, which is viewed

as a biblical command and each Witness is required to submit a monthly 'Field Service Report' on their progress.

The future?

The state of the Church of England

Why would you want to become part of an institution like the Church of England? Isn't religion an old/dying cult event?

It's true you hear a lot of this these days. That religion is outdated and outmoded, and is on the way out. It goes hand in hand with a position that lots of people hold – that they are 'spiritual but not religious'. To be 'religious' is something constraining and negative, rather than the positives that might be found in being spiritual. Let's be honest, some forms of religion are indeed negative. They reject questioning attitudes, and force unquestioning obedience in thought or action. But that's not what I see in the Church of England. Its breadth allows it to enfold a number of different points of view and ways of expressing spirituality. It gives me space to follow and worship God without forcing me to adopt beliefs or activities that don't fit me.

Nor is the Church of England in decline. It's a story we often hear told, that the numbers of church attendees are dropping, but the most recent evidence shows that the Church is actually growing at a gentle rate. Religion may be old, but it's certainly not dying. Yes, many churches in the West are declining in numbers, but there are more that are growing. Outside the UK the picture of growth is even more marked, with places like Africa or China experiencing the exponential growth of religion in general and Christian churches in particular. I think religion serves a need in us as human beings, to bring us to a recognition that there is something greater than us, something upon which we depend for our existence. More than that, being a community, it gives us a framework of support and guidance in which to live our lives.

I'm happy to become part of an institution like that, one that serves others in showing them the way to God through the love of Jesus, and serves God in showing his love, acceptance and encouragement for all people.

And you think the Church of England really looks like that, do you?

Hah. Well, yes, that is an ideal picture. That's what the Church should look like – what I hope it is growing into, and what I hope I and other Christians can represent. Of course, the world and reality being what they are, the ideal isn't the reality. There are plenty of less-than-perfect churches, vicars and Christians out there. Our job is to work to make the ideal into the reality.

The Anglican Communion

What's the difference between the 'Church of England' and 'Anglicanism'?

Anglicanism is a broader term – it includes more than just the Church of England. The term originally referred to the Church of England alone, and arose during the second half of the seventeenth century. But then as Britain began to explore and colonise other parts of the world, it spread its Church to those places. Thus you can find 'Anglican' churches throughout Africa, India, Sri Lanka, Canada, Australia and New Zealand. The United States of America calls its version of Anglicanism 'The Episcopal Church', but it's still Anglican, and part of the wider whole. All together, these churches are known as the 'Anglican Communion', and send their senior clergy to meet together at the Lambeth Conference, held every ten years.

As you might expect from a body that is spread all over the world, the churches of the different regions don't always see eye to eye. At the moment they especially don't.

Yes, what's that all about? There's lots in the news at the moment about the Anglican Communion falling apart.

This is the coming to a head of a conflict that's been a while in coming. There is a profound divide between the Anglican Churches of the northern and southern hemispheres. In the southern hemisphere, especially in Africa, all denominations of Christianity are thriving and growing like never before, Anglican Churches included. There are so many Anglicans spread throughout the world now that statistically the average Anglican is a young, African woman: probably not what you might think of when you think of Anglicanism! But despite their large numbers, there seems to be a feeling among Anglicans in the southern hemisphere that their voices aren't heard by their sister churches in the North.

Recently this has come to a head in the conflict over homosexuality in the Church. A great many Anglican churches, especially in the southern hemisphere, are in places where the cultural atmosphere is massively homophobic, to the extent that it's not uncommon for gay people to be prosecuted, imprisoned and killed. In general, the Church in those places doesn't support violence (although there are exceptions to this rule), but it certainly holds that homosexuality is a sin.

Meanwhile the Anglican churches in the northern hemisphere have been becoming progressively more liberal, including with regard to homosexuality. In 2003 the American Episcopal Church made an openly gay priest a bishop, crucially, without first discussing the move with the other Churches in the Anglican Communion. For the southern Churches, this was a huge slap in the face. Their beliefs were known and yet ignored. And what was worse, there was a resulting anti-Christian backlash in their own countries, which associated Christianity with homosexuality, and thus made all Christians fair game for violence. A gay bishop was ordained in America, and Christians were beaten unconscious elsewhere as a direct result.

*But wasn't the American Church doing something good that
needed doing?*

I think so, but the problem is it isn't as easy as that. Actions
have consequences. While the northern Churches become
more liberal and progressive, they are effectively asking
southern Christians to suffer for them. If they then take
further progressive steps without even discussing them with
the people who will suffer in consequence, it's understandable
that those southern church leaders will fight back.

Fight back how?

The most recent Lambeth Conference was held in 2008.
Four Anglican primates (the heads of Anglican Churches in
nations outside England) from Nigeria, Uganda, Kenya and
Rwanda, refused to attend in protest against the actions of the
Episcopal Church. Their boycott was joined by the Archbishop
of Sydney and the Bishop of Rochester.

Instead they held their own conference in Jerusalem a
month prior to the Lambeth Conference, calling it the Global
Anglican Futures Conference, or GAFCON. It was attended
by numerous conservative Anglican clergy, who made it clear
that they felt they were no longer fully connected to either the
Church of England or The Episcopal Church.

The threat was implicit: if things get any worse, this
division would only get deeper.

So what's happening now?

The previous Archbishop of Canterbury, Rowan Williams,
did his level best to keep everyone together. He proposed an
'Anglican Covenant', designed to make sure that if any of the
Communion's member Churches decided to do something
radical without consulting the other members of the
Communion, they would suffer disciplinary action. However,
although the Covenant was well received in some regions, it
ran into problems when voted on by churches on the extreme

ends of the liberal/conservative divide. For the liberals, it was too hard-line. For the conservatives, it wasn't hard-line enough. Sadly, even in the Church of England, it was voted against in the majority of the dioceses.

No one is sure what will happen next. The hope is that our new Archbishop of Canterbury, Justin Welby, will be able to lead us towards a new solution to this extremely prickly problem.

Do you think the Anglican Communion will split?

I honestly don't know. In a way I hope not, because there are enough splits in the Christian Church already without adding another to the pile. But on the other hand, the division is deep and real hurt has already been done on both sides. I'm not sure what could bring together two groups which are so diametrically opposed. We'll see what happens next.

How can the Church be so divided about gay people?

I'll tackle that question in the chapter on ethics a bit later.

The Worship of the Church of England: What we do and why we do it

Types of worship

What does 'worship' actually mean? What does it entail?

The word 'worship' comes from the Old English *worthscipe*. Literally it means to give worth to something. In the context of Christianity it indicates the act of asserting that God exists and is worthy of our recognition, through our response to that fact.

What a response to an awareness of the greatness and generosity of God might look like can comprise a vast range of options. It might involve prayer, singing, reading aloud, silence, listening to others, or any combination of those things. It might be done by a lone individual, by a group, and with or without a designated leader.

Do you worship the cross?

No. I understand why you might think that: after all, crosses are prominently displayed all over churches and Christians often have a cross in front of them when they pray. But we don't worship the cross. It's more of a memory aid, or a focusing device. It gives us something for our eyes to rest upon while we're trying to open the rest of our minds.

When Christians wear crosses around their necks or as lapel badges they're simply using them as an identifier – something that says 'I'm a Christian'.

Is 'worship' the same thing as services?

Services are a form of worship. Certainly, when one thinks
of worship in the Church of England, one tends to think
of formalised services of worship, most usually on Sunday
mornings.

What kinds of services are there in the Church of England?

Services can be divided up into three categories: eucharistic
services, non-eucharistic services and occasional offices.

Eucharistic services

What does eucharistic mean?

'Eucharist' literally means 'thanksgiving' in Greek and it refers
to the service that may also be called Holy Communion, Mass
or the Lord's Supper. Within the Church of England all these
different names are used for this service, with people choosing
which term to use depending on their tradition, and that of
the congregation as a whole. So you might find one Church of
England church offering 'Mass' services, while another might
be offering services of 'the Lord's Supper'. Names aside, they
all refer to the same service, centring upon the taking, blessing,
breaking and sharing of bread and wine. They will also all have
the same indispensable elements, according to church law.

Eucharistic services need at least one other person besides
the priest leading the service to be present, and some priests
would insist on at least two others being present. This is a
response to Jesus' promise that he would be present 'where
two or three are gathered in my name' (Matthew 18:20).

What does a eucharistic service involve?

There are several elements that by law have to be included in a
Eucharistic service. These are:

- a greeting
- prayers of penitence – these are prayers where the congregation calls to mind their sins and expresses remorse for them. According to church law, the service must use a version of these prayers that has been authorised by the General Synod
- the Collect – this is the special prayer of the day, with a different one provided for each Sunday
- two readings from the Bible, of which one must be from the Gospels
- a sermon
- a creed or affirmation of faith (as above, has to be an authorised version)
- prayers of intercession
- a Eucharistic Prayer (as above, has to be an authorised version)
- the Lord's Prayer
- breaking of the bread
- distribution of Holy Communion
- some kind of blessing or words of dismissal.

Often, but not always, a eucharistic service might include hymns, songs or some other form of music.

What's a creed?

A creed is a statement of what we believe as Christians, which the whole congregation recites together. Creeds at the minimum contain statements of belief in: God the Father, who created everything; God the Son, Jesus Christ, who was made incarnate, born, died and was raised; and God the Holy Spirit. The Church of England uses three authorised creeds: the Nicene Creed, the Apostles' Creed and the Athanasian Creed. All three come from the early Church, where they were created in response to all the debate around the nature of God and of Jesus.

What's a 'Eucharistic Prayer'?

It's the prayer that includes the consecration of the bread
and wine. There are several authorised versions, but they all
involve: a calling to mind of the story of what God has done,
from Creation, through Christ's life, death and resurrection to
the present day; a specific recalling of the Last Supper; and the
four separate actions of taking, blessing, breaking and sharing
the bread and wine.

The 'Last Supper'?

This is the event remembered in all four of the Gospels when,
the night before he was arrested, Jesus celebrated the Jewish
Passover with his disciples. In the Gospels of Matthew, Mark
and Luke, Jesus takes, blesses and breaks the bread and says
'This is my body'; then takes, blesses and shares the wine
saying 'This is my blood'. This is the bare bones version we
find in Mark's Gospel. In Matthew and Luke we get a little
more detail, and Jesus tells his disciples that they are to do
this same action 'in remembrance of me'. Christians began
to perform the ritual of Holy Communion in response to this
command from Jesus, and it was already an established part of
Christian worship by the time Paul was writing his letters – 60
CE at the latest.

What happens when the priest blesses the bread and wine?

Different parts of the Church of England believe different
things about what actually goes on during a Eucharist, so I'll
try to answer that in the next chapter on belief.

*Are the bread and wine made specially? Where do you get them
from?*

They don't have to be made specially. A lot of churches get
them from professional church supplies vendors though, at
the same time as they're buying candles or whatever else

they need. But if I turned up to take a Eucharist service and discovered there was no bread and wine waiting for me, it would be fine for me to nip down the shops and pick up a bottle of wine and a loaf. What we can't do is use something *other* than bread or wine and use it as a substitute. I couldn't use milk instead of wine, for example. It has to be wine (although it can be non-alcoholic).

I thought a lot of churches used little papery wafer things instead of bread.

Plenty do. It's a lot easier and more hygienic to hand out individual wafers rather than rip a piece of bread apart on the spot. They're made out of wheat (gluten free are available), so 'count' as bread. Still, I've also worshipped in churches that used big loaves of bread. It just depends on the feeling of the church where you're worshipping.

What's on the altar during eucharistic services?

It depends on where the church is on the spectrum of church tradition. In a middle-of-the-road church during a eucharistic service you will generally begin with at least two candles, the service book, perhaps a free-standing cross being on the altar. At a particular point in the service, the priest leading the service will set up the vessels for the Holy Communion. These would consist of:

- A white cloth called a 'corporal', on which the vessels are laid.
- At least one 'chalice' for the wine. Chalices are traditionally made out of silver and look like big goblets.
- The 'paten', is a small silver plate on which the bread is laid.
- A 'pall'. This is a stiff cardboard square covered with white linen which is laid over the chalice to prevent dust and so on getting into the wine.

- A 'purificator'. This is a white cloth folded into a long narrow strip, which is used to wipe the chalice after someone has drunk from it and dry the vessels after they're washed at the end of the distribution of the bread and wine.
- Some churches use a 'burse' and a 'veil'. A burse is a little square fabric covered folder in which corporal and purificators are placed. The fabric's colour will reflect the colour of the season. A veil is a large square of cloth, again in the colour of the season, which lies over the top of the chalice. The burse goes on top of the veil. They're used to cover up the vessels used for Holy Communion when the chalice and paten aren't in use.

Why silver for the chalice and paten?

For purely practical reasons. Silver has antibacterial qualities, meaning it's easy to clean and doesn't harbour germs. With so many people sharing the same cup, germs are a real concern.

How do I know whether to receive the bread and wine during a Church of England service?

You should feel welcome to share in the bread and wine at a Church of England service if you're a confirmed member of the Church of England, if you're used to sharing in bread and wine at your home church (of any other denomination), or if you're both baptised and desiring to be confirmed in the Church of England. There's a conversation happening at the moment about welcoming people to share in the bread and wine who have been baptised but not confirmed, including children, but that's still a matter of debate. If in doubt, either go up to the place where the bread and wine are being distributed and bow your head for a blessing, or just stay where you are in the congregation.

Do I have to come up to the altar rail to receive the bread and wine?

It depends on the church. Look and see what other people are doing, or follow the directions of the team showing people where to go and when. Some churches like people to kneel at the altar rail to receive the bread and wine, some like you to stand, some have more than one place where the bread and wine are being distributed. Just follow the example of the regulars!

What should I do when I get there?

If you wish to receive the bread and wine, bring your hands up in front of you, palms upward, with one hand under the other making the shape of the cross. The person distributing the bread will either place it into your crossed palms, or indicate that they want to place it straight into your mouth (depending on the tradition of the particular church). They will say some words to you as they give you the bread, usually along the lines of, 'The body of Christ keep you in eternal life'. You then say 'Amen' and eat the bread. Receiving the wine follows the same basic process. Keep your hands up and make eye contact with the person carrying the chalice. When they say the words of distribution, say 'Amen'. Depending on the tradition of the church, the chalice-bearer might hand the whole chalice to you to take a sip, let you hold the bottom of the chalice to control the tilt while they hold the stem, or place it to your lips without you touching the chalice at all.

If you want a blessing, keep your hands down and your head bowed. The priest will take this as a sign to offer a blessing.

Non-eucharistic services

Do 'non-Eucharistic' services cover every other kind of service?

Apart from occasional offices, yes. However, there's not all that many of them. As the name suggests, non-eucharistic services are worship services that don't involve Holy

Communion or any other kind of sacrament. There are four
public church services offered by the Church that come under
this heading. They are: Morning Prayer, Evening Prayer,
Compline and a Service of the Word. All can be led by non-
ordained leaders, although such leaders always need to be
licensed by the local bishop for this ministry. All four types
of services include: a greeting; some kind of praise, be that
a hymn, a song or a set of responses; at least one reading
from the Bible; a creed or affirmation of faith (must use an
authorised version); prayers, including the Lord's Prayer; and
some form of blessing or dismissal to end.

Compline?

This is a late night prayer service, sometimes simply called night
prayer. In religious communities, and in my theological college at
least, Compline heralds the 'greater silence'. That means that
after the service has finished, there is to be silence throughout
the night until after Morning Prayer the next day. Compline is
designed to be the last act of worship before going to bed. It sets
you up for the night, just like Morning Prayer sets you up for
the day. Even if most places other than religious communities
can't keep the great silence, Compline still marks the end of the
day, and congregations are encouraged to go home and to bed
immediately after it concludes.

What's a 'Service of the Word'?

A Service of the Word, unlike the other services which have
quite prescribed forms, comes almost entirely in the form
of notes and directions for local churches to do what they
like with them. It allows lots of variation and choice and is a
popular option for churches that don't want to offer eucharistic
services every Sunday or who like to have a particular local
flavour to their services. Besides the elements listed above, a
Service of the Word also must include prayers of penitence
and a sermon or talk.

I've heard of a couple of other services you haven't mentioned here. What about 'Matins'? Or 'Evensong'?

'Matins' is an older name for Morning Prayer. Usually if the church uses this older title they'll be using the older version of the service too, from *The Book of Common Prayer* (*BCP*).

'Evensong' is a variation on Evening Prayer. It has all the same elements, it's just that a lot of those elements will be sung, there will be more in the way of hymns, and there will almost certainly be a choir.

Unlike eucharistic services, this range of non-eucharistic services can be performed even if the person leading the service is the only person there.

Occasional offices

So what are 'occasional offices'?

These are services for special occasions (hence 'occasional'), namely baptisms, confirmations, ordinations, marriages and funerals. These can all involve Holy Communion, but don't have to.

Is it called baptism or christening? Is there a difference?

Nope, no difference. When we're talking about infants, exactly the same service could be called either a baptism service or a christening service, although 'christening' would be an informal term. If we're talking about adults, the service would only ever be called baptism.

What does it involve?

The service will usually be included in your local church's regular Sunday worship. The Church of England encourages this because one of the key things that's happening when you're baptised is that you're joining the Church. If baptisms occur in special private services it's easy to lose sight of that fact. That said, some churches do offer private services all the same. Check with your local church.

Within the Church of England we baptise both babies and people who are old enough to make their own faith decisions. There are two authorised services, one in the *BCP*, the other in *Common Worship*, but both involve the following elements:

- The Presentation. Here if the person to be baptised (the candidate) is old enough to speak for themselves, they declare their desire to be baptised. If the person to be baptised is a baby, the parents and godparents are asked to declare their intent to bring the little one up as a Christian and within the Church. The congregation responds by declaring their intention to uphold the candidates in their new life.
- The Decision. Here the candidate or the parents and godparents on behalf of an infant, declare their intent to turn away from evil and sin and towards Christ, in the form of six questions and responses.
- Signing with the Cross. The minister performing the baptism makes the sign of the cross on the forehead of the candidate or the infant, using a specially blessed oil, as a sign that they have been claimed for Christ.
- Prayer over the Water. The minister blesses the water to be used.
- Profession of Faith. The whole congregation reads out an affirmation of faith.
- Baptism. This can be done either with a font or with a baptismal pool. If using a font, the candidate leans over the font, or the minister holds the infant over the font, and water is poured on their heads while the minister says the words of baptism: '*Name*, I baptise you in the name of the Father, and of the Son, and of the Holy Spirit. Amen.' If using a pool, the candidate either has water poured over their whole body or, if the pool is deep enough, their whole body is dipped into the water three times while the prayer is spoken.

This is followed by the minister saying a prayer of blessing.
* The Commission. This is a piece of instruction delivered by the minister performing the baptism, reminding everyone of what baptism means, and concluding with a prayer for grace and protection for the newly baptised and their families.

Who can conduct baptisms?

Normally only an ordained person can conduct a baptism. Usually this would be a priest, but deacons can take baptisms too. The exception is in the situation of an emergency baptism, when absolutely anybody, provided they are baptised themselves, can conduct a baptism.

'Emergency' baptism?

Yes, in situations when the person to be baptised is seriously ill, or definitely about to die. Sadly, it's something that occurs relatively frequently with babies, and hospital chaplains, and on occasion nurses, find they are called upon to baptise newborns who aren't expected to live.

Is that something to do with wanting the babies to avoid going to hell?

I'll go into what we believe baptism does and belief about life after death in the section on belief. For now suffice it to say that sometimes parents are worried about that, but, speaking as a priest, it's not something I'm concerned might happen.

Can someone perform an emergency baptism without getting permission?

Absolutely not. The parents *must* request an emergency baptism, and vicars are expressly taught that we are to make clear to them that questions of ultimate salvation or of provision for a Christian burial do not depend on whether the baby has been baptised.

Why baptise babies?

We perform baptisms for several reasons: to thank God for the gift of life; to start the baptised person on their new life of faith; and to bring the baptised person into the Church and to give them the church community's support and prayers. All of these apply every bit as much to babies as they do to adults.

But isn't baptism about making a decision to become Christian? Don't you need to be old enough to make that decision first?

You could argue that. There are plenty of Christians out there, Baptists most notably, but also people within the Church of England, who think baptisms should be adult-only affairs. It means that when a person is old enough to make their own decision to follow Christ they are able to mark and celebrate that decision in the form of baptism. I know a number of adult Christians who were baptised as babies and regret that now because they never got to mark their own decision/conversion in that most important of ceremonies.

However, I and those who support infant baptism would argue that blessing babies and welcoming them into the Church is a valid action. An adult decision to follow Christ can be celebrated and marked in the service of Confirmation, where candidates reaffirm the promises made at their baptisms, are blessed by the bishop, and usually receive Holy Communion for the first time.

If they want to be, can't people just be baptised again as adults?

No. Once you're baptised, you're baptised. There is a service that the Church can do, called an Affirmation of Baptismal

Faith, in which baptised people can reaffirm the promises made at baptism and either be sprinkled, or sign themselves, with water from the font. But if you're already baptised, the Church really shouldn't baptise you again.

Shouldn't? Don't you mean won't?

No, unfortunately. There are some churches who will re-baptise, but they shouldn't, and are contravening church law to do it.

What do you do if someone wants to name their baby something inappropriate at a baptism service?

A service of baptism isn't a naming ceremony. Babies have already been legally named by the time their parents take them to church to be baptised. On this basis, even if the baby's name is something odd that might raise eyebrows, a vicar doesn't have the right to try to make changes at that stage. Baptism is about welcoming the child into the Church, not giving them a name.

The exception to this position is when the parents want their baby named in the service with something blasphemous or obscene. In that situation we would be justified in asking the parents to have a rethink.

Can anyone get married in a Church of England church?

Yes, as long as you're a heterosexual couple. That's one of the things about being an established Church. If you want to get married in your local church, by law the vicar has to oblige, regardless of your attendance record or personal beliefs. However, if you or your spouse-to-be is a foreign national it's a little more complicated. In any case, you also have to be able to prove that you have a qualifying connection to the church in which you want to get married.

A connection? Like what?

The Church actually wants to make it as easy as possible
to get married in a church, so many things count as valid
qualifying connections. The official list includes:

- the parish where you live
- the parish where you were baptised or confirmed
- a parish in which you have lived for six months or
  more, at any time during your life
- a parish in which you have attended worship for at
  least six months at any time
- the parish in which your parents lived or worshipped
  (as long as it was during your lifetime)
- the parish in which your parents or grandparents
  were married.

Why is being a foreign national a problem?

There have been a number of cases recently where people
have had sham marriages to make it easier to get residency in
the UK. There has even been at least one vicar sent to prison
for presiding over sham marriages. The Church has therefore
advised its clergy that foreign nationals should be married after
common licence rather than banns. This means that there's
more paperwork involved, including the collecting of more
information and the couple swearing an affidavit that the
content they've provided is true.

Can people be married at whatever time of day they like?

Nope. By law we can only take marriages between eight in
the morning and six in the evening. You can get married on
any day of the week, though, as long as the vicar has no other
commitments for that day/time.

Can you take a marriage outside?

Again, that's a no. We can only take marriages inside churches.

Can vicars conduct civil partnership ceremonies?

No.

Can you bless civil partnerships?

We're not supposed to. But given that vicars can and do bless all manner of other things, from flags to pets, plenty of vicars find ways to be able to pray for and/or bless civil partnerships depending on their personal feelings about such partnerships.

Can you preside over the marriages of people who have been divorced?

We can now, although it is down to the conscience of each individual vicar as to whether they will or not.

For myself I'm happy to marry people who have been divorced once, but the marriage preparation session will be quite in-depth, and I will ask questions about what went wrong, what has been learned, and what will be different this time around. If people have been divorced more than once, it's a much tougher decision, and can only be judged on a case-by-case basis.

What happens if someone tries to stop the wedding when you get to the 'if you have any reason why these persons may not marry you are to declare it now' bit?

There are only four possible reasons that are accepted as grounds to stop the wedding. They are:

- At least one of the couple is under the age of consent, or is aged 16–18 and doesn't have parental permission for the wedding.
- One of the couple is misrepresenting their sex, making it an attempt to have a same-sex marriage.
- The marriage would constitute incest.

- One or both of the couple are already married to someone else.

If someone stands up during the wedding saying they have a reason why it needs to be stopped, the minister would pause the wedding proceedings, take the person into a private room and find out their reasons. Nothing apart from one of those four possibilities above would count. Even if the person insists that one of those four things is the case, they need to be prepared to pay the cost of the wedding in the event that they're not telling the truth. Traditionally, they have to be prepared, then and there, to pay in cash.

Has it ever happened to you?

No, thank goodness! I've got a good few years ahead of me though, so it may do yet …

The liturgy

Why do services have particular things that they must include?

The simple answer is because the General Synod has told us that they have to. The more complicated answer is because we're trying to do particular things in and with services.

First of all, the Church of England as a whole is interested in being as true as it can be to the roots of Christianity. We want to get close to Jesus, what he did and what he asked us to do, and we want to get close to what the earliest Christians did when they worshipped. Scholarship, especially recently, has uncovered quite a lot of material about how various early Christian communities worshipped, the words they used and so on, and all the Christian denominations have made efforts to use this new information to shape how we worship today.

Secondly, services are aimed to have an effect. Different services have different effects they're seeking to achieve, but they are all looking to move people emotionally and spiritually and bring them closer to God. So the best services have a flow, a rising and falling, with space for people to think and breathe and catch their balance. They have time set aside for looking at God's word and thinking about it, in the shape of readings and a sermon. They have a place reserved for thinking about our failings and asking for forgiveness. They have places kept for asking God for what we need and for praising him, reminding ourselves why God is worthy of our devotion. And finally, all services are designed to send people out on a high note. To get all that, we need to include all those elements stipulated by the General Synod.

Who writes the services?

There are three sources of authorised material for worship in the Church of England. The first is *The Book of Common Prayer* (*BCP*). Versions were published in 1549 and 1552, written and edited by Thomas Cranmer. Later amendments were added in 1559 and 1662. These days we use the 1662 version. Cranmer, as we saw in the last chapter, was one of the leading lights of the English Reformation, and the *BCP* is almost wholly his work.

The second source is the small library of books that together are called *Common Worship*. It was put together by the Church of England's Liturgical Commission, authorised by the General Synod and published in 2000. It's made up of nine books, each of which addresses a different area of worship.

The third source was also written by the Liturgical Commission and was published at the same time as *Common Worship*. This is *New Patterns for Worship*, which gives some more experimental ideas and prayers for use in the Church.

It's worth adding at this point that although the *BCP* doesn't allow for much variation, *Common Worship* has lots of options and different versions of prayers, blessings and so on for particular points in the Christian year. This wealth of options means that each individual parish can put together its own perfect mix of the various different parts, and, in fact, is allowed to adapt and rewrite certain parts of the service if it wishes.

What's the Liturgical Commission? Who's in it?

The Liturgical Commission is a permanent commission of the General Synod. It prepares forms of service, advises on the development of liturgy, exchanges information and advice on matters of liturgy with other Churches (Anglican and otherwise), and promotes the development and understanding of liturgy.

It currently has 19 members, although this number can change. I won't list names here, but they can be found on the Church of England website if you're interested. For now I'll just say that the members are not all ordained, and are all well-respected experts in the history, development and practice of liturgy.

What's the 'Christian year'?

Over the course of the year, the Church celebrates different events in Jesus' life at different points. For the Church, the year begins with the period of Advent on Advent Sunday, the fourth Sunday before Christmas. This is followed in order by the seasons of Christmas, Epiphany, Lent, Easter, Pentecost, Ordinary Time and for some (but not all) the Kingdom Season. Each season is marked by different prayers, different coloured fabrics used around the church and for the priest's vestments, and different elements added to or removed from services. It adds up to give a sense of movement through the year, and ideally a sense of travelling with Jesus as we remember certain times and events in his life.

I've heard of some of those, but not all. Can you break them down?

Sure.

- **Advent**: colour is purple (or an alternative is a blue known as 'Sarum blue'). This colour indicates a season of waiting and preparation, and the content of the services often reflects this more sombre atmosphere. In the case of Advent, we're waiting and preparing for Christmas, and the coming of Christ. During purple seasons the Church will no longer say or sing the Gloria – a song glorifying God which begins, 'Glory to God in the highest and peace to his people on earth'.

- **Christmas**: colour is white or gold. These colours are used for the Church's most holy days and times, and indicate full-on celebration. Obviously at Christmas we're celebrating Jesus' birth at Bethlehem.

- **Epiphany**: colour is white or gold. This season covers the period after Christmas, beginning with the celebration on 6 January of the arrival of the three wise men to visit Jesus and ending with the festival of the Presentation of Christ in the Temple on 2 February. 'Epiphany' celebrates God revealing himself in Jesus Christ, hence the celebratory colours.

- **Lent**: colour is purple. Again, this is a waiting and preparation season, as we get ready for the big celebrations of Easter. As with Advent, the *Gloria* isn't sung, and this season there is also a prohibition on using the word 'alleluia'.

- **Easter**: colour is white or gold. This is perhaps the biggest celebration of the Christian year, as we celebrate Christ rising from the dead. The Easter season lasts for 50 days.

- **Pentecost**: colour is red, signifying flames. This is when we celebrate the gift of the Holy Spirit in 'tongues of fire' a few days after Christ's return to the Father.

- **Ordinary Time**: colour is green. Ordinary Time is actually all the Sundays where we are not celebrating or preparing for something else. There are a few weeks of Ordinary Time between Epiphany and Lent for example. Ordinary doesn't mean 'normal', though. It's from 'ordered' and means days which are 'counted'.

- **Kingdom season**: colour is red. This season is optional, and whether or not to celebrate it is left to the discretion of each parish. Some churches don't keep it, preferring to keep the green of Ordinary Time. It begins the day after All Saints' Day and runs through to the day before Advent. Its highlight is the festival of Christ the King, a celebration adopted by the Church of England from the Roman Catholic Church, who began celebrating it in direct opposition and provocation to Mussolini and Fascism back in 1925.

How are lay people involved in services? What are they allowed to do and when?

As I mentioned earlier, the Church is its people. Jesus didn't write a book or found a great building: he brought together a collection of people. The Church is the spiritual descendant of that first group of believers. So it makes sense that the Church's worship isn't just about who stands at the front. All Christians, lay and ordained, participate fully in the worship and life of the Church. Lay people can do everything in a service apart from absolving people of their sins, praying the Eucharistic Prayer, and offering the final blessing. For some parts of the service, though, the lay person must be trained and licensed before they can do them. Preaching, leading services and distributing Holy Communion all require either a licence or permission from the diocesan bishop.

Some churches like to keep lay involvement at a minimum, while others involve lay people as much as they can. In rural parishes, where there may be a large number of churches and very few clergy, it's often necessary for there to be a high level of lay involvement, since the vicar won't be able to make every service. In my experience it's normal to have lay people doing intercessions and readings and carrying the wine during the distribution of Holy Communion.

What sort of music is used in church? Which is better – organ and full choir or guitars and tambourines?

Ah, a loaded question! To answer the first part, music in churches can run the gamut between no music at all to massed choirs or rock bands. When music is used, the range from church to church, and even within individual churches, is enormous.

Of the music options you might find, the first is of course no music of any kind. Some Christians find music an active distraction when trying to experience God's presence, and so appreciate simple or contemplative services at which there is no music or singing.

The second option comprises various types of singing. This might be chant or plainsong, which is usually associated with monks; it could be singing psalms, which is rarer these days, but you may find it at services of Matins or Evensong; and it will almost certainly involve singing hymns or songs, which is almost the default for most Church of England services these days. These hymns might be very old or very new, they might have a contemporary 'rock' type sound using a worship band, or they might be more traditional, making use of organs or other traditional instrumentation. The music on offer will usually vary according to the church's place on the spectrum of church tradition and the nature of the service. Services trying to appeal to young people, for example, will often make a conscious decision to use more modern songs.

Finally there's the option to have instrumental music with no singing. This is quite rare in my experience, and is usually only used at the beginning and end of services, and to fill gaps: for example, when the preacher is climbing the pulpit steps, or while the priest is preparing the altar for Holy Communion.

As to whether modern or traditional is 'better' … I don't think either one is intrinsically better or worse. There are some stunning traditional hymns, and there are some wonderful new hymns and songs written to be played by bands. Equally, there are some horrendous, theologically dubious and trite hymns, and some vacuous and dull modern worship songs. The trick is to take the best of both worlds, and make sure that the gathered clergy and congregation are going to find them spiritually helpful rather than something that will make their ears bleed.

Who decides when during a service you should stand, sit or kneel?

There's no hard and fast rules on whether or when you should do any of these things. The *BCP* specifies when you should stand, sit and kneel, but these days it's not normal for congregations to follow all those instructions, however much they may be fans of the traditional service.

You don't have to kneel to pray. Everyone these days thinks it's traditional, but in fact it isn't the oldest prayer posture. Originally people would either pray standing, often with their arms raised to heaven, or if they knelt they would abase themselves entirely, adopting a posture we're probably more used to seeing in images of Muslims at prayer. The 'kneeling up on hassocks' kind of prayer posture is a medieval development and reflects a feudal understanding of God as a King to whom worshippers should kneel in homage.

I should also say at this point that what people do at which point in the service is largely down to local custom, so it's by no means a big problem if you're new in a church and you find yourself sitting when everyone else is standing. People understand that this stuff is idiosyncratic and you're not a mind-reader. Plus, if the vicar didn't announce what you should be doing at that point, then they've got no one to blame but themselves.

At theological college it was felt that everyone should do what they felt was right for them at each point in the service. This meant that there were times when some people were standing, some sitting and some kneeling. It looked untidy, but sometimes tidiness isn't the greatest of virtues.

All of that said, generally it's normal to stand at the beginning, during the hymns (because it's really hard to sing sitting down), during the Gospel reading and the first half at least of the Eucharistic Prayer (although it could be argued that the best practice is to stand throughout), and at the end.

What position should you adopt to pray?

It really doesn't matter, as long as you're consistent. Whatever physical position you choose for prayer, it is a good idea to choose a particular way to place your body. Just as people will kneel or seat themselves in a certain way to meditate, the same holds true for praying. What you do with your body will affect what you do with your mind, and focusing is easier if praying is done with a regular accompanying physical posture.

So, are the Church of England's services all designed for large congregations?

By no means. The Church also has services and prayers written for much more intimate situations, such as one-to-one confession and absolution, healing services, prayers for the dying and prayers of blessing.

Isn't confession a Roman Catholic thing?

Well, yes, the Roman Catholic Church certainly does offer one-to-one confessions, but so does the Church of England. It's just a lot rarer for our churches to have confessionals or similar obvious clues that we might offer confession (although a few do!). Since the Church has public confession as part of every eucharistic service (where we call to mind our sins and ask forgiveness for them), many people don't feel the need for private confession. But some people really need the experience of telling another human being their sins and being assured of God's forgiveness. That's where confession – which in the Church of England we call a service for 'The Reconciliation of a Penitent' – comes in.

Since many people don't know that the Church of England offers confession, it tends to be something that is either specially requested or specially offered. Only priests and bishops can hear confessions and offer absolution.

Are prayers for the dying the same thing as Last Rites?

Essentially, yes. In the Church of England the prayers for the dying don't have to involve anointing with oil, but equally well they can. It's always a tremendous privilege. You come to the dying person's bedside, at home or in the hospital, hold their hand, and pray for them. Often they die very soon afterwards. Sometimes the person is not fully conscious, while at other times they can be absolutely conscious and wanting to receive Holy Communion or make their confession.

Do you do exorcisms?

The Church of England does do exorcisms, but not very often. For a start, individual vicars don't do them. If a situation does emerge which seems like it might call for an exorcism, vicars are under strict instructions to refer the case up to a diocesan specialist in these kinds of things, who is known as a specialist in 'deliverance ministry'. Even then, an exorcism will only take place with the express permission of the bishop and following a psychiatric assessment for the person requesting it. This is because of the enormous possibility of making things worse rather than better, especially if the problems experienced stem from mental illness.

I'm told by other vicars that although exorcisms per se may be relatively rare, it isn't uncommon to be asked to bless a house or an individual where 'strange' things have been happening. This is a much lesser action than an exorcism, and simply involves praying with and for people. There is even a short recommended service for this kind of ministry in *Common Worship*.

Do you believe in ghosts, then?

I can't say that I either do or don't. I don't know. I know for certain that some people are sure they've experienced paranormal things, and I know some vicars who are sure they've encountered these kinds of oddities and made them better with prayer. I haven't experienced anything like that yet, but I'm not foolish enough to assume that I never will. I try to keep an open mind and not worry about it too much.

Prayer

You've mentioned prayers quite a lot, but I'm not sure I'm clear on what a prayer actually is.

To pray is always to put oneself in God's presence, but can also include communicating with God and, in the case of 'intercessional' prayer, asking God for things. Prayers can be said out loud by many people, said out loud by one person on behalf of many people, said out loud by one person for themselves, said silently inside one person's head, and can even involve being silent inside and out and just listening. Prayers don't always require words!

However, in the context of church services, the main body of prayers are intercessional, which is to say that someone will pray out loud for the whole congregation, and ask God for particular things. Traditionally, prayers of intercession will involve praying for the Church, the world, the local community, those who are sick or suffering and those who have died.

Does it work?

A wise spiritual adviser once said to me that God always answered prayer, but there were three possible answers: yes, no and wait. It's a fact that people don't always get what they pray for. Some of these prayers we might expect God to give a firm 'no' to, such as prayers for personal gain, or for harm to come to someone else or suchlike. But other prayers are not guaranteed positive responses either.

That said, a great many prayers are answered with a 'yes', and although I've not personally seen or experienced a dramatic healing, I know very trustworthy people who have.

Some of my prayers almost always receive positive answers from God, particularly prayers for courage, for faith, and for the wisdom to say the right words into difficult situations. Similarly, prayers for strength and peace for others often seem to be answered with a resounding 'yes'.

Why would God not say 'yes' to prayers asking for others to be healed?

I don't know. But I think that, firstly, all of us must die at some point, and something must cause that death. Sometimes an illness or injury is the thing that will cause a person's inevitable death. Secondly, there is more to health than the purely physical. In the Church these days when we pray for healing we often pray for 'wholeness', understanding that God might want to be healing a person's mind or spirit rather than their body alone.

What I emphatically do not think is that some people aren't healed because they are being punished. I don't believe for a second that God acts in that way.

You say prayers for changes to your state of mind are often answered. But isn't that just you fooling yourself?

I suppose it might be, but I don't think that's the case. Yes, I think God can and does act to affect my state of mind. I'm sure that they are the kind of changes that would show up if I was being brain scanned while I was praying. That doesn't mean I'm the one causing those changes. I certainly don't think that changes to my mental state *have* to be a result of me somehow talking myself into feeling a certain way. The state of my physical brain affects my thoughts and mood. At the same time, my thoughts and mood affect my physical brain. When God communicates with me or bestows mental courage or peace upon me, absolutely I think that will change the state of my physical brain too.

Do you think prayer could act as pain relief?

I suppose that if you're spiritually practised enough to be able to shift your mind into a truly meditative state then it could. I really don't think this kind of meditative prayer is practised often enough by your average Christian for me to recommend it in general, though. If in doubt, stick with a doctor's prescription.

Where does the Lord's Prayer come from?

It shows up in two of the four Gospels: Matthew and Luke, in a slightly different form in each. The version of the Lord's Prayer that we use most often in the Church of England today is the longer version from Matthew, with an additional verse of praise (known as a 'doxology') at the end.

It's called the Lord's Prayer because it is the prayer Jesus used when he was asked to teach his disciples to pray. Every service of worship in the Church of England has the Lord's Prayer in it somewhere.

Why do we always say 'amen' at the end of prayers? What does it mean?

It's a transliterated Hebrew word, which is used to show agreement with a preceding comment or speaker. It's usually translated as 'truly' or 'so be it'. It's used quite a lot in the Old Testament by people wanting to agree with a previous speaker, and Jesus uses the term in the New Testament like that but also in a new way, at the beginning of a statement to emphasise its truth. This appears as 'verily' or 'truly' in English translations. Using 'amen' to show agreement to praises and prayers is a common feature in the letters of the New Testament, and so the Hebrew word stuck around into modern usage.

Do you use rosary beads in the Church of England?

Some of us do. Traditional rosary beads consist of ten smaller
beads in a number of sections, each divided by one larger bead.
From one of these larger beads comes an extra strand with a
crucifix at the end followed by a larger bead and a number of
smaller beads. The idea here is that on each smaller bead you
pray a 'Hail Mary' ('Hail Mary, full of grace, the Lord is with
thee; blessed art thou amongst women, and blessed is the
fruit of thy womb, Jesus. Holy Mary, Mother of God, pray for
us sinners, now and at the hour of our death. Amen'), and on
each larger one you pray the Lord's Prayer.

There are also specifically Anglican rosaries, which consist
of twenty-eight smaller beads in four groups of seven. These
four sections are each separated by one larger bead, and the
extra strand consists of a crucifix and just one extra larger
bead. Rather than simply praying Hail Marys and the Lord's
Prayer, other prayers can be substituted.

In both cases, the desired effect is the same: that you
pray in a settled rhythm, allowing your fingers to keep count
of which prayer comes when which sets your mind free to be
open to God. I've never known rosaries to be used in services,
but as an individual spiritual aid they can be very useful.

*What can a service give that can't be gained through private
prayer?*

There are two basic answers to this question. First, it gives
a sense of community. Our prayers aren't just about us as
individuals and God, they're about us as a community of
believers working together in God's service.

Second, it provides a useful spiritual discipline. Some
people can maintain amazing spiritual discipline, praying fully
and deeply every day, upholding strict routines of reading
Scripture and so on. Unfortunately, I believe these amazing
people are in a minority. I certainly appreciate being called to
a set place at a set time to hear Scripture, hear that Scripture

expounded, and pray with others. It gives me a spiritual shape and rhythm that I might not otherwise achieve on my own.

What does 'hallelujah' mean?

It's another Hebrew word. Strictly it's an exhortation to praise addressed to several people as in '[Everyone] praise him!' 'Alleluia' is the same word, but transliterated from the Greek transliteration of the Hebrew. In modern usage, and in the book of Revelation, 'hallelujah' is an expression or word of praise in itself, rather than an exhortation to others to praise.

Movement in worship

In some services I've seen people crossing themselves. I thought that was a Catholic thing? Why do it?

We do this in the Church of England too, especially in churches and for people on the Catholic end of the spectrum of church tradition. For people from High Church traditions crossing oneself is pretty common. It's an embodied prayer which calls to mind two main things:

- the Trinity, with the threefold crossing-self movement indicating Father, Son and Holy Spirit
- the cross on which Jesus died.

High Church people who wish to will often cross themselves at certain times during services:

- at the beginning and end of services and often at the beginning of sermons in response to the invocation of the Trinity, i.e. 'In the name of the Father, the Son and the Holy Spirit'
- when the Gospel is read
- when receiving forgiveness of sins after the prayers of penitence
- in response to being blessed

- during the Eucharistic Prayer at the *Benedictus qui venit* ('Blessed is he who comes in the name of the Lord'), and some choose to cross themselves at the words of institution as well (which conclude with 'Do this in remembrance of me')
- just before receiving Holy Communion
- when calling to mind the resurrection from the dead during the Creed.

I've seen people bowing during services. What's all that about?

Bowing, or its more extreme cousin, genuflecting, are actions practised by Anglican Christians on the higher end of the spectrum of church tradition, and there's a few reasons why they might do it during a service. Firstly, it's customary to bow (also known as 'to reverence') to the altar whenever you either stand in front of it or walk past it. This is a sign of respect for its role in services of Holy Communion – in that it is the place where the bread and wine are blessed. While the Church in England was still a part of the Roman Catholic Church, it was common for a relic to be incorporated within an altar – a relic being one of a saint's bones or personal items or similar things, which would be the focus of such reverencing. These days altars tend not to have relics within them in Church of England churches, but the practice of bowing continues.

Secondly, people might bow at the mention of Jesus Christ during prayers and the reciting of the Creed, or at points when the Trinity (Father, Son and Holy Spirit) are mentioned instead of crossing themselves.

Thirdly, people might bow to the bread and wine immediately after they've been blessed.

What does genuflecting look like?

It's like a really low curtsey. Your right foot goes back, you bend your knees until your right knee touches the floor, hold that position for a moment, then straighten back up. It's like a super bow.

In the Church of England, does the priest ever kiss the altar?

In churches with a High Church tradition, they often do, yes, as well as kissing the Gospel before it's read. It's a gesture of reverence and respect.

The million-dollar question

Why go to church? Can't you just live a good, honest life?

I hope and trust that people come to church because it helps them to do just that. The implicit assumption in the question reflects the pervasive idea in western culture that belief and spirituality are private. Our beliefs sit in our heads in some kind of personal bubble that needn't, and indeed shouldn't, be revealed or shared with anyone else. The cult of individualism that's grown over the centuries tells us that we should do just fine on our own, that we should build our own private relationship with God, and we should form and uphold our own ideas of ethical behaviour as individuals.

But the thing is, we human beings are social creatures. Even the most introverted of us needs human contact at some point, because we build our identities in relationship with other people. 'No man is an island entire of itself', as John Donne would have it. Belief and faith are never held in isolation. They are always shaped and swayed by the beliefs and attitudes and questions of those around us.

What church is supposed to do is to provide a safe, nurturing space for our faith. It allows us to be part of a community of people who believe the same core things. It gives us a place to reinforce our faith in several ways: by being in the presence of other believers and speaking and sharing matters of belief with them; by receiving teaching from the scriptural readings and sermon; by having space in which to

pray, by being lifted by singing and praise; and above all by
spending time in God's presence. The Eucharist is particularly
important, for me at least, because it is the ultimate expression
of the fact that we are a single community, bound together as
we share one bread and one cup of wine. We're not alone. If
church does what it should, when we emerge from a church
service we should feel part of a larger whole, energised and
empowered to live that good, honest life with God's help.

I know plenty of people who have never set foot inside
a place of worship and are the most honest and upstanding
people you could hope to meet. It is possible to lead a good,
honest life without going to church. I just think that church
makes it easier.

Christian Doctrine: What we believe and why

A quick word of warning before I get into questions about what Church of England vicars, and Church of England Christians in general, believe. Even in a Christian denomination that sets great store on all of its members believing the same things you will find a great range of beliefs and opinions. Within the Church of England, which is a self-consciously broad church, that range is enormous. I'll try to be as even-handed as possible, making it clear when my personal answers differ significantly to what you might find elsewhere, but there just isn't space in this book to survey the full range of answers that Church of England vicars might give to questions about belief.

My answers will primarily reflect my own personal beliefs. Given my background as a student of theology and my personal stance as a liberal Christian, you can expect responses that fall on the liberal end of the liberal–conservative spectrum. Just be aware that there are certainly Christians out there who will believe quite different things to me, and that's fine!

Doctrine in a broad church

Isn't it problematic that one Church holds lots of different beliefs?

It can be, in that there are plenty of questions about belief on which Anglican Christians can't see eye to eye. It also makes it harder to present a clear image of what the Church believes and what it is about to non-Christians. Periodically the church leadership worries about the Church of England's lack of a single unified doctrinal system, but as yet we've not found a way to gain that doctrinal unity without sacrificing our inclusivity. Faced with that choice, thus far the church leadership has decided it's more important to keep everyone together than it is to make sure everyone believes exactly the same things.

If you all believe different things, how can you say what's true?

This is the thing. As you'll see when we come to questions about what God is like, Christians believe that God is infinite, eternal and measureless. By definition, there is no way that humans can even begin to appreciate what God is like. Theology always has to be done with the caveat that even the language we use for God is going to fall woefully short of the reality. I think if theologians are honest, we have to accept that even our most carefully crafted ideas about God might be way off the mark, and it's our responsibility to re-craft our theology when we're faced with clear evidence that we've got something wrong.

In light of all that, it's really hard to talk about truth as if it were something we could nail down without a shadow of a doubt. We can't. It's just not possible. God's too big for us to nail down anything about him. All we can do is hold tight to the truth about God's self that he showed to us in Jesus Christ. Christ is the yardstick against which all subsequent divine revelations (because Christians believe that God continues to reveal himself in the world even now) and theological work must be measured.

All the same, I don't think God minds if we get the details wrong. As long as we live the life asked of us by Jesus and keep trying to understand God better and draw closer to him, it's the intention that's important. What that life might look like I'll go into in more detail in the next chapter, but, as I understand it, the key point is that our beliefs shouldn't ever be used to hurt others. As for the truth about God, everything will be made clear to us in the end. As Paul put it in his first letter to the Corinthians, 'For now we see in a mirror, dimly, but then we will see face to face. Now I know only in part; then I will know fully, even as I have been fully known' (1 Corinthians 13:12).

If you're so sure you're not going to get near the truth, why bother trying to work it out?

For me it has to do with a right response to God. When he was asked what the most important commandment was, Jesus replied that it was to love God and to love your neighbour as yourself. But he described loving God in at least three different ways, listed in different orders depending on which Gospel you're reading. My favourite version comes from Mark's Gospel: '"you shall love the Lord your God with all your heart, and with all your soul, and with all your mind, and with all your strength".' As I understand it, loving God with my mind involves me trying to understand more about him and his plans for me and for the world. I know I may get things wrong, and since it needs correction time and time again, the work of theology may never be finished, but I know I have to try. I want to know God. I believe he reaches out to us in the person of Jesus, and the only right reaction to that is to reach back.

The Bible

Do you believe every word of the Bible is true?

It depends what you mean by 'true'.

That everything in the Bible literally happened.

Some Christians believe that. I don't. I think that to assume that every word in the Bible must refer to something that literally happened is to misunderstand the nature of the book.

For a start, the Bible isn't one homogenous mass. It's more an anthology. It was written by many different people at many different points in time and for a wide variety of different reasons. Just in the Old Testament there are books devoted to detailing the Jewish Law. There are books all about the history of the Jewish people. There are books of prophecy. There are poems and writings about wisdom. Comparatively few of these genres are interested in what literally happened at a given point in history. In fact, I'd say the ones that are are in the minority. I'll say more about this as we go along.

You do believe some of the things in the Bible actually happened, though? Like what?

Yes, I do. The New Testament as a whole is pretty solid for me. I think there may be exaggerations, or incorrect dating, and there are slightly different words and details from one source to another, but without picking apart each instance, which would take a long time, I'm happy saying I think most of the events recorded in the New Testament happened.

The Old Testament is a lot more complicated because so much of its content happened so very long ago. Some of the oldest portions of those Scriptures are at least three thousand years old, and that's only when they were written down. The stories themselves were certainly circulating orally prior to the writing itself, and that process of telling and retelling could have taken any amount of time. We just don't know enough. That length of time means it's hard to get close to the events recorded. Archaeologists, particularly in Israel itself, are working hard to find some kind of objective evidence for biblical events, but it's a long, slow process, and thus far there hasn't been a lot found that matches directly with events as recorded in the Bible.

That said, some things do seem to connect. There seems to have been a period in the history of that region where there was a sudden influx of people and building projects. This might connect with the Exodus story of the Hebrews leaving Egypt and invading the area we now call Israel. We also know

that the Egyptians cast out large groups of their population
at other points in history, so they may have done the same
thing with the Hebrews. Unfortunately, there is no Egyptian
archaeological evidence for this particular group leaving,
although we know the Egyptians later tangled with the people
of Israel.

Later on, events such as the invasions of Israel by the
Assyrians and Babylonians are well attested by the invading
nations as well as there being archaeological evidence that
backs up the biblical account. The later the history is, the more
likely it is to be an accurate historical representation.

Do you think anything in the Bible definitely didn't happen?

Some of the stories in the Bible are definitely apocryphal –
told not because they accurately reflect historical events, but
because they convey a truth about God's relationship with
his people and vice versa. So the story of Jonah, for example,
isn't history. Nor is the story of Job. The book of Genesis in
particular contains myths about pre-history that while I don't
think they actually happened as recorded, hold important
truths about God's relationship with the created order. (I'll
explain what I mean by 'myth' in the section on Creation.
For now, it's important to remember that to say something is
myth is not to say it is untrue.)So, no, I don't think God created
the world in six days in 4004 BCE. But I do think he created
the universe, space and time. There'll be more about that in
the next section about the doctrine of Creation. I don't think
the story of Noah is historical truth. There may have been
a massive flood in the Ancient Near East that might have
inspired such stories, but I definitely don't think there was an
ark, or the drowning of the whole world.

The very early stories of God's people from Abraham
onwards feel more like gathered stories than history to me,
all the way through to the settlement of the land we now call
Israel. But I don't think we have proof either way, so I can't say
I think any of that definitely didn't happen.

Why is the Bible divided into the Old and New Testaments?

The Old Testament is made up of the Jewish Scriptures, albeit in a different order than is used by the Jewish people themselves. 'Testament' is another word for 'covenant' and means a binding agreement. The Old Testament therefore refers to God's first binding agreement and relationship with humanity, that is to say, with the people who came to be known as the Jews.

The New Testament, on the other hand, refers to God's new relationship with humanity, which Christians believe was inaugurated by the birth, life, death and resurrection of Jesus Christ. Thus the books of the New Testament were all written in or after the first century, and were all written by followers of Christ.

Why did Christianity keep the Old Testament?

There was a large and protracted argument about this in the early days of the Church. One school of thought held that the Old Testament no longer had anything to say to followers of Christ, since Christ's appearance, what he did and said, superseded anything written for the old faith. The most extreme manifestation of this point of view was found in the various shades of Gnosticism. The Gnostics held that the Old Testament wasn't just no longer relevant, but that God as recorded in its pages didn't refer to the one true God at all. They believed the God of the Old Testament was indeed the creator of the world, but that the world was flawed, and its creator was an evil demi-urge. Obviously, with this kind of view, they thought the Old Testament should be utterly rejected.

That doesn't sound like such a bad idea. I mean, God seems to do lots of awful things in the Old Testament. He doesn't really match up with the 'love thy neighbour' God of Christianity.

That's certainly the impression that it's easy to take away from the Old Testament. It's an oversimplification, but there are

multiple books of the Old Testament, particularly Exodus and
history books like Samuel and Chronicles, that characterise
God as much more anthropomorphised than the God we see
in the New Testament. He has negative emotions. He can
be angry, jealous and vindictive. He holds grudges. And most
obviously, he is faithful to one race over another. This to the
extent that to give the ancient Jews, the Hebrews, the land
which he promised them, he empowers and commands them
to wipe out the original inhabitants of said land utterly. The
God of love this does not seem to be.

But there are two things which we have to bear in mind
when we read the Old Testament. First, the Old Testament
was written and revised by many different people over many
centuries. The Hebrews' understanding of who their God
is and what he wants from them changes visibly over time.
I feel comfortable in suggesting that although the writers of
the various books of the Old Testament were writing about
their relationship with God, their own understandings and
motives colour the text (as indeed is the case with the New
Testament). So when the God of the Hebrews was thought
of as being one god among many, the writers of that period
write of him and his people as competing against other gods
and the people of other gods. God is *theirs*, and they were *his*,
so it would be quite right for him to be on their side as they
attempted to conquer and subdue their land. In the same way,
when the Hebrews, now calling themselves the people of
Israel, found themselves attacked and subjugated by the great
empires of the Assyrians, Babylonians, Persians and Greeks
in succession, they needed to understand that in the light of
their relationship with their God. So we get books of prophecy
that explain why all this awfulness was happening: because
the people of Israel had broken their promises to God, and this
was his punishment for them. Who the writers are, and the
events that surrounded them, impact on the picture they paint
of God.

Second, this vindictive view of God is only one of a vast
range of images of God that appear in the Old Testament.
There are also tender images of God, as a shepherd, as a

mother, as a parent teaching his children to walk. God also appears as supremely mysterious: in the burning bush, when he tells Moses his name is 'I am that I am', when the writer of Psalm 139 describes the experience of God as being knowledge 'too wonderful for me; it is so high that I cannot attain it'. The negative stuff is only one side of a complex, rich, mysterious collection of images of God. These multiple images of God in the Old Testament are facets of the truth which is too great for us to grasp all at once. Each illuminates another side to a being who is too far beyond us for humans to ever fully understand. With this in mind, it's easier to see how focusing on a single image to the detriment of others will give us a warped idea of who God is and how he interacts with the world.

Finally, we need to add to this the Christian idea that the Old Testament cannot be understood without the New Testament. As those early Christians who argued so hard against the Gnostics had it, the Old Testament is like half a story, pointing forwards to its climax which is Christ. To understand the Old, you need to look through the lens that is Christ's person and teaching. He's the final piece that makes the jigsaw make sense.

But isn't it just confusing, then? Why not just stick with the final image? Wouldn't that be easier?

Maybe, but it would also be incomplete. Jesus was a Jew. He read the Jewish Scriptures, he worshipped in the synagogue, he understood his own mission as being promised and described in those Scriptures. In Matthew's Gospel, during the Sermon on the Mount, he describes himself as the 'completion of the law'. Jesus saw himself as the final point on humanity's long journey to learn more about God and to draw closer to him.

The journey is important. It tells us about humanity as much as it tells us about God, and most of all it tells us about the relationship between the two. These are things we all, Christians most definitely included, need to know. Knowing how people respond to God, and how he responds to us is, I would argue, far more important than knowing the exact details of the ancient history of the Jewish people. Which is just as well, because as I mentioned above, the Bible isn't all that interested in revealing concrete historical details. It's all about the relationship.

What do you do about the internal contradictions in the Bible?

If we're working on the basis that the Bible doesn't always contain literal historical happenings, I don't think internal contradictions need to be a problem. The spiritual usefulness of the Bible doesn't stand and fall on how tight its internal logic might be. It is important that we're honest about the existence of contradictions, though. Any attempt to gloss over that kind of thing is disingenuous at best and actively harmful at worst.

Why are there even internal contradictions in the first place?

Again, there are two answers to this one. The practical answer is because of the multiplicity of writers and sources. Theologians who specialise in studying the Bible have many different tools for understanding the text better. One of the older tools they can use is a practice called 'source criticism', which was developed at the end of the nineteenth century. This works on the assumption that the reason there are contradictions, repeats and occasionally full-on confusion in the Old Testament is because the final form of its books is made up of overlapping layers of multiple sources that have been edited together over time. So, for example, there are two creation stories in Genesis, and they differ from each other in pretty fundamental ways. One shows male and female humans being made at the same time, with nothing to choose between them, while the other has the woman being a secondary creation, made out of Adam's rib to be a helper for him. Source criticism says that each of these stories was written at a different time, by a different person, with different understandings and motivations at work for them in their writing. If two people tell the same story, chances are there will be differences and contradictions.

There's also a spiritual answer. One of the problems many Christians have with the fact that contradictions exist in the Bible is that they find it hard to reconcile such 'flaws' with the idea of the Bible being the 'word of God'. Why would God bring about the existence of a book that seemed to include mistakes, repetitions and conflicting accounts? However, I think we can argue that God might deliberately allow the flawed humans writing their accounts of their experiences and relationships with him to tell their stories in different ways, and to make their own mistakes. In so doing he would make sure that his followers wouldn't lean too heavily on the Bible as a source of authority. The Bible would be important, certainly, but only God himself would and could be the ultimate source of truth.

Who wrote the Bible?

As I said above, many many people have contributed to the Bible over the millennia. Even books that seem to have one obvious author, like the prophetic book of Isaiah, for example, was most probably written by at least three major writers, contributing their sections at different times in Israel's history, and then was probably edited further by any number of later scribes and members of schools of prophecy. There are too many possible authors to list them all here.

Really, within the Bible there is only one author who we can name and be absolutely confident we know a fair amount about. That author is Paul of Tarsus. Not all the letters attributed to him in the New Testament are definitely his, but some are. From them we know quite a lot about who he was, what he was doing and why he was writing, which is a refreshing change!

Were the writers of the Gospels members of the twelve disciples of Jesus?

In one case at least, we know he wasn't. There wasn't a 'Luke' among the Twelve. As for the others, the short answer is we don't know. However, bearing in mind that if Jesus died around 33 CE and the first Gospels were being written down around 60 CE at the earliest, that would make the disciples pretty old to be writing Gospels. Getting to a reasonable old age was rarer in those days, especially when we consider that the early followers of Jesus were suffering persecution, and many of them died young. It's more likely that the Gospels of Matthew, Mark and John were written by authors close to the earliest disciples, rather than the disciples themselves. That said, as far as I can see that doesn't make them any less informative or insightful.

   We also have to be careful about falling into the trap of thinking that there can only be one holder of a particular name. 'John' must be John the brother of James, for example. All these names were extremely common in the ancient world, and there's nothing to say that the authors of the various books and letters weren't using pen names (as was a common practice at that time) to attach additional credibility and authority to their work.

Did Moses write the first five books of the Bible?

No. Not least because Exodus records his death. Running through those five books known by the Jews as the Torah: Genesis, Exodus, Leviticus, Numbers and Deuteronomy, biblical scholars believe there are at least four major strands of authorship. Source critics have named these strands with letters: J for Yahwist, E for Elohist, D for Deuteronomist and P for Priestly, each one of these named for the characteristics within the text that mark them out. These strands are understood to originate from quite different time periods: from the ninth, eighth, seventh and sixth (or fifth) centuries

BCE respectively. Definitely not all originating with one person, then.

When was the Bible written?

Different bits were written at different times. Some of the early books, like the Torah, as I mentioned above, are made up of interwoven strands of different written sources, so it's impossible to give a definitive date. The best we can do is offer an estimate for when the book took its final form. A caveat: all biblical dating is still very much a matter of scholarly debate and, even when estimating, estimates can vary wildly from expert to expert. I've tried to go for majority scholarly consensus here.

Old Testament:

- Genesis, Exodus, Leviticus, Numbers: final versions eighth century BCE
- Deuteronomy: c. 625 BCE
- Joshua, Judges, books of Samuel, books of Kings: c. 625 BCE
- Isaiah (in three distinct sections):
  - chapters 1–39: c. eighth century BCE
  - chapters 40–55: c. sixth century BCE
  - chapters 56–66: c. sixth to fifth centuries BCE
- Other prophets: various dates ranging from eighth century BCE to fifth century BCE or even later
- Psalms: vast range, as the psalms were written by many different people for many different purposes. They range from c. 950 BCE to c. 70 CE
- Daniel: probably the latest book in the Old Testament at c. 165 BCE
- Other writings (Proverbs, Ecclesiastes, Job etc.): a range of dates again, but probably no material earlier than sixth century BCE, and most cluster around fourth century BCE.

New Testament:

- Matthew, Mark, Luke: 60–90 CE
- John: 80–95 CE
- Acts: 60–90 CE
- Earlier letters: cluster around *c*. 60 CE
- Later letters: cluster around *c*. 100 CE
- Revelation: 60–100 CE.

Is that it? I've seen Bibles with some other books included.

Ah yes. Those are the books the Church of England refers to as the 'Deuterocanonical Books' or the 'Apocrypha'. There are 18 books in all, encompassing a variety of different genres. Biblical scholars think these were largely written in the 'intertestamental period' in the last couple of centuries BCE and the first century CE. The question of whether these books are part of the biblical canon proper is a matter of debate. Protestants generally hold that they are not, while Roman Catholics and Eastern Orthodox Christians hold that they are. The Church of England, with its mix of traditions, tends to leave that question up to the individual worshipper. To make it more complicated, the Church of England also includes three books within the 'Apocrypha' that other denominations do not recognise as 'Deuterocanonical books'. Within the Church of England, however, the terms are interchangeable.

When were all these different bits combined into the Bible we know today? Who chose which went in and which didn't?

The books we now regard as biblical 'canon' were recognised by three different church councils in succession in the late fourth century CE. These were the Council of Laodicea (363), the Council of Hippo (393) and the Council of Carthage (397).

It's important to say that the bishops attending these councils didn't just pick and choose which books they liked, though. The list of the books to be regarded as canon sprang first and foremost from knowing which books Christians commonly used already. If it was debatable whether a book was already commonly used, the council attendees discussed whether it should be included.

So although the bishops at these councils underlined which books were included in the Bible, their decisions really reflected the existing state of affairs.

How did they decide which debatable books should go in?

There were several areas to be thought about. Was the book written by an apostle, or someone close to an apostle? Did the Church at large make use of the book? Were the contents of the book consistent with the beliefs and teaching in the more central Christian texts? Was the book of a high spiritual or moral value? All of these areas were considered, debated and prayed over.

What's the difference between an apostle and a disciple?

The only difference is whether we're speaking about them before Jesus' death and resurrection or after. Jesus' followers were known as his disciples while he was still around and teaching, but after his death, resurrection and ascension, they were known as apostles. This is to reflect what they were doing. 'Disciple' means 'follower' or 'student'. 'Apostle' means 'someone sent forth'. While Jesus was around, they were learning. When he had left, they had been given their marching orders and were out doing his work.

Did (or does) everyone agree on the list of books that the councils produced?

Through the centuries various theologians have had problems with the more debatable books. Martin Luther, for example, thought the Letter of James should be struck out of the Bible. Despite these occasional issues, most Christians happily accept the official canon.

Do you believe the Bible is the word of God? What does that mean?

Yes, I do.

What that means will vary from Christian to Christian. For me, it means that the books of the Bible were inspired by God. They all record some response to God's presence and actions in the lives of people. So when we read the Bible we can experience the flow of God's power and presence through time, and discover what he reveals about himself to us through that presence.

What it emphatically doesn't mean is that God whispered words into the ear of the author who then wrote it all down verbatim. The books of the Bible are written in the words of human authors and, although are written in response to the divine, are human work. So they include human motives, understandings, editing processes and so on. There will be flaws and mistakes, and unedifying glimpses into the social and cultural mores of certain time periods.

For me, the Bible being the word of God is a two-stage thing. The first stage is the author writing about his (in the case of the Bible the author is always a he) experience of God's power and presence. The second stage is me reading the author's words. For the Bible to truly be the word of God to me, I need consciously to be reading it in God's presence and with his help. That way at my spiritual best I can see past the mistakes and through the cultural assumptions to the truth of what God has to say to me. All of which makes reading the Bible a form of prayer.

Do you think the people who view the Bible as a literal piece of instruction are in danger of idolatry?

I think it's a danger, yes. Worshipping the book and not the power shown through the book would make that book a literal idol, and skew subsequent thinking about what God shows us and the methods by which he reaches out to us.

The Bible is a dangerous book. It's dangerous because it carries with it great power and authority, and in the wrong hands it can be used to hurt and destroy. Such great power demands careful and prayerful handling. Unfortunately, using the Bible as a literal piece of instruction can be pretty much the exact opposite of such careful and prayerful handling, particularly when it's used to hurt or oppress others.

The flip side to this, of course, is that when that great power and authority is used carefully and prayerfully, following Jesus' example, it can be the most wonderful source of freedom, strength and comfort.

What do you think about Christians using quotes from the Old Testament Law to justify modern moral stances?

I'm dubious about it. During his Sermon on the Mount, Jesus said he had not come to abolish the Law, but called himself its 'end' (or 'completion' or 'fulfilment'). For me, following the thought of St Paul, what this means is that as a Christian I'm not bound by that bare Law any longer. Instead, I'm bound by Christ. What Christ teaches, I'm bound to follow. Where he directly contradicts the Law, I follow his new teaching. Where he's silent on a matter of the Law, I consider that the Law no longer holds and I am left to decide my own course with reference to the two 'greatest' commandments: to love the Lord my God, and my neighbour as myself (or, as John's Gospel has it, to love others as Jesus loved me). What the bare Law has to say about something comes a very distant second to these first considerations.

What about Christians using Biblical quotes in general to justify their moral stances?

There is a practice known as 'proof-texting', whereby a person finds a biblical quote that taken out of context might seem to back up their argument, and then use that as 'proof' that they're correct. It's not a practice restricted to one or other end of the liberal–conservative spectrum; it can be done with the New Testament as much as the Old and is an unhelpful and misleading practice. As I said above, the great power of the Bible demands prayerful handling, including considering the context of the words and the spirit of Christ's new commandment to love one another.

Creation

Creation: literal beginnings of man and the universe or an analogy to help people better understand?

Before I put forward my own beliefs, it's important to note that there are Christians out there who do indeed think that the creation stories in the Bible are literally true. I'm not one of them. I don't think they detail the concrete literal beginnings of humanity and the universe. The two creation narratives in the first chapters of Genesis aren't even direct analogies, I don't think. Rather, they are myths.

Myths? You mean they're made up?

No, not quite. Myths aren't literally true, but they contain a core of truth that informs how we understand the world. Myths in the context of the Bible won't reflect literal historical events, but will have something spiritually useful to say about God's relationship with and attitude to humanity and the universe as a whole.

So the image that the writers of the creation stories in Genesis use of created matter as being a vast dome called 'sky', surrounded by water above and beneath – I don't think that's literally the case. I don't think there are many Christians around these days who would argue for that being the case. But the image of the Earth and its atmosphere being an isolated bubble of space where humans might live – that rings true to me.

Can you believe in God and dinosaurs at the same time?

Yes. If I'm not invested in the idea that the creation stories are literally true, that means I don't have a problem with the idea that creatures not listed among the created order in Genesis lived on the earth at some point. Nor do I have a problem with the idea that it might take a lot longer than seven days for creation to reach the stage it has presently reached.

But the dinosaurs became extinct. Wasn't that kind of a waste of time?

Only if you're working with a very linear view of what is a good use of time. Are bacteria valuable? Are plants? Do things only merit their existence if they contribute towards the development of humanity? I don't think so. I believe everything has its own intrinsic value and is valuable to God, dinosaurs included. Humanity may become extinct at some point in the future. I don't think that would make our period of life a waste of time, or make us any less children of God and loved by him.

What do you think about evolution versus creation?

I accept that evolution is still a theory at the moment, and its details are still being fine-tuned by biologists. But currently it's still the best working theory we have. On that basis, I think it does a good job of explaining how that particular facet of the universe works, and needs to be incorporated into how we understand the world. I don't think there needs to be an 'either–or' mentality going on here. 'Creation' doesn't automatically mean 'creation in seven days literally as set down in Genesis'. All that the term implies is that there was a situation when time and matter didn't exist, and that a Creator brought them into existence. With this stripped-down definition of creation, it has no problem sitting side by side with the theory of evolution.

If evolution is just an automatic process of survival and reproduction, where's God in all that?

I believe God works with his creation in many different ways. I don't see why evolution couldn't be one way of doing that. If God knows everything, he would know the outcome of a process of evolution within the framework of the universe he created. If his final aim was to create humanity, he could easily have designed the process and the framework in which it operates so that it would give rise to humanity.

What makes humanity so special?

I know, right? Why us? You look around, at the sheer scale and awesomeness of the universe, and you can't help but feel very small indeed. But in the face of this, the Bible tells us in the Genesis creation myths, in the Psalms, and more than anything else, in the story of Christ, that God wanted humanity in particular, that he loves us and wants us to love him back. That he loves us enough that he would come to us in our own form to experience the world as we do and to save us from ourselves. It blows my mind every time I think about it.

Without reference to God's self-revelation through the biblical authors and through individuals through the millennia, I'm not sure we'd be able to think of humanity as particularly special. This is one of those cases where faith comes into play. We believe that we're special because God tells us that we are.

Why would you change how you think about the process of creation in response to a scientific theory? Aren't you sure you've got the right answers?

I firmly believe we're being dishonest if we aren't prepared to revisit conclusions in the light of new ideas, even conclusions that have fitted well with our faith in the past. Faith doesn't exist in some kind of bubble away from the real world. Faith means that we believe that God is real, and his interactions with the world are real. So then, if he is real, nothing that we discover or theorise about the rest of the world needs to be troublesome or threatening. We should be able to incorporate those new discoveries into the lattice that is our picture of the universe as a whole, and its relation to its Creator.

We don't know everything there is to know about God. So we don't know everything there is to know about how God acts in and relates to the world. As we learn new things about the universe, that will tell us a little more about how God relates to it. Science and religion are two ways of looking at a single reality, with each illuminating the other. Just as science advances as new discoveries build on old theories, so theology has to move forward too.

When people are ordained in the Church of England, they are called upon to make the 'Declaration of Assent', which basically involves accepting the beliefs, practices and governance of the Church of England. One part of the declaration recognises the Church's call to proclaim its faith 'afresh in each generation'. For me, a crucial part of this 'afresh' is to allow our theology and faith to develop as our understanding of the world develops.

The Bible doesn't talk about the universe – only the Earth. Is that a problem?

No. Although there's obviously a focus on the Earth because that's where we live, I don't see why the creation story can't equally apply to the universe as a whole.

What about other worlds? What if there are aliens?

Again, I don't think the existence of other worlds or life on other worlds would cause difficulties for the belief that God created the universe. The original creation stories aren't being exclusive by speaking only about this world. This world is the only world they knew about, and so they were being inclusive, speaking about everything they knew. It makes sense to me that as our world-view expands we can understand the creation stories as expanding too.

Would aliens existing cause problems for the idea of Jesus saving the world?

More about this in the section on Jesus!

God

Do you really believe in God? All the time?

Yes. All the time. I would be a useless priest if I didn't.

I've heard about plenty of vicars who've lost their faith.

It does happen. Being a vicar doesn't make you immune to doubt, and there have been, and will be, vicars who find they no longer believe in God. Often it seems to creep up on people, and often it goes hand in hand with clergy burnout. A clergyperson is working harder and harder, running themselves into the ground, and then one day they look up and realise they're just about holding the day-to-day business of the parish together, but they're doing it by rote. There's no sense of God's presence and support any more. That person might be an excellent administrator or manager, but, as a priest, losing touch with God takes away their ultimate purpose.

What happens when you find you don't believe in God any longer?

The important thing, for that vicar and for the parish in which they serve, is for them to recognise that loss of faith as soon as possible and stop just soldiering on. Something has to change. For some people, the loss may be a temporary thing, caused by overwork and loss of perspective. For them, they need a programme of spiritual recovery. This might include taking time off, taking a lengthy spiritual retreat, scheduling regular sessions with a spiritual director or just generally making space for themselves and God. All of these things can and do recharge depleted spiritual batteries.

For others, the loss is lasting. For them they need to leave the Church's service and find a new line of work. You simply cannot be a vicar and not believe in God, because in that way lies dishonesty and long-term damage for both them and for their congregations.

What do you believe God is like?

The first thing to say is that I believe God is a Trinity.

Trinity?

The Christian belief that God is three in one and one in three. God is Father, Son and Holy Spirit.

Isn't that just three Gods?

No. God is one God.

So you believe that one God has three parts?

Again, no, not really. The Father, Son and Spirit aren't 'parts', as if they were parts of a body. Nor do we believe they are different faces of the same God.

That makes no sense.

That's not an uncommon viewpoint! The Trinity is one of the hardest things for any Christian to get their head around, and I think most of us never really manage it. We have one Sunday a year dedicated to the recognition that God is Trinity – Trinity Sunday – and I suspect most vicars dread it because it means talking about the Trinity to the general puzzlement of the congregation.

Often vicars try to use visual metaphors to help in thinking about the Trinity, like the famous example of the shamrock, which is one plant but with three sections, or the example of water sometimes being liquid water, sometimes ice and sometimes steam. The problem is, all these metaphors fall short.

The Church has spent centuries arguing about how we could believe in one God and yet believe that there was a Creator God, but that Christ was also God, and then that the Holy Spirit was God. In the early Church there were two opposing extremes of thought about how all that could work, with a spectrum of ideas between them. On the one side was 'modalism'. This was the belief that the Father, Son and Spirit were three masks or appearances of the one God. The other extreme was 'tritheism'. This was the belief that God was actually three Gods. The early Church decided that both these extremes were heresies, and ever after has tried to sail a middle course between the two, with varying degrees of success.

The thing is, Christians believe that God is infinite, ultimately unknowable (at least as we are now) and mysterious. Our systems of reason and logic will never be able to sum up a being like that. Any attempt to sew up a definition of God in a neat logical package will simply not work. This is why so much language about God in theology and worship is paradoxical. That's the only way we can express a truth that is at its heart inexpressible. The Trinity is a Mystery with a capital 'M' – one of the areas of Christian faith in which words will always fall short of the reality.

Why would you want to struggle so hard to talk about God being a Trinity? Isn't it just something Christians have made up?

It's not something made up. We believe that the Trinity can be seen throughout the Bible, and crucially in the lives and experiences of believers. So, in the Old Testament for example, God is spoken of in the plural form in Genesis. In the same book we see reference to the 'Spirit of God' – *ru-ah* in Hebrew, literally meaning 'breath' – as 'moving over the face of the waters' at creation. The wisdom literature of the Old Testament (Proverbs, Ecclesiastes, Job, Song of Songs), in books like Proverbs, speaks of 'Wisdom' as a personified aspect of God, often gendered female. In the New Testament we see Jesus praying to God, referring to God as Father, and claiming for himself a number of different names including 'Son of God'. In the prologue to John's Gospel we see an amazing picture of the 'Word' of God (who is clearly identified as Christ) as being God, present and effective in creation, but then taking on human form. At the end of Matthew's Gospel we find the 'Great Commission': the command from Jesus to go out and baptise people 'in the name of the Father, and of the Son, and of the Holy Spirit'. The Trinity is definitely there.

Can't you just say that there are three Gods?

No. The Bible is equally clear that God is one. It's a message that runs throughout the Old and New Testaments, and Jesus himself quotes 'The Lord your God, the Lord is one' from Deuteronomy as the starting point of the greatest commandment.

So how do you talk about this, if it's basically impossible to express in words?

Theologians traditionally refer to the Trinity as three 'Persons' with a single 'substance', although the term 'Persons' could also be replaced with terms such as 'modes of being' as the Reformed theologian Karl Barth has it, or 'distinct modes of subsistence' as the Roman Catholic theologian Karl Rahner prefers to express it.

Where Christian theologians agree is on the fact that each of the Persons of the Trinity is an active force (so no thinking of the Holy Spirit as a 'thing', for example), and just as in themselves the Trinity are three, so all three show themselves in and through God's involvement with the world. Their inward being reflects their outward actions. There is no hierarchy in the Trinity, so it's not as if the Father comes first, then the Son, then the Holy Spirit. All the Persons have always existed and will always exist, and no one of them is superior to either of the others.

To explain how these three Persons are one, Christian theologians hold that they are of one substance, a word which could also be translated as one nature or essence. Different theologians put forward different theories for how the unity of the three is expressed. One theory is that of 'perichoresis', where the three Persons are engaged in mutual indwelling or 'co-inherence'. Each one permeates the others, in perfect intimacy. Another is that of the 'social Trinity', where the unity of the three is in the closest fellowship imaginable.

As I'm sure you can tell, there is no consensus among Christians as to how this all works. It is possible for virtually every formulation of the doctrine of the Trinity to be dismissed as one or other of the two heresies of modalism or tritheism, and the debate continues, as I suspect it will do until the point where God finally makes himself fully known to us.

Until then, all that Christians can agree on is that God is three and one, Father, Son and Holy Spirit, and that how that can all be is a Mystery. But then, God is the infinite Creator of all time and space. It's not all that surprising that we can't sum up his being in a neat phrase or two.

So apart from being a Trinity, what's God like?

To start with, we only know what we believe God has shown us about himself. Some things we can see from the Bible, in what God has said and done in the history of his involvement with the created order. Some things are hinted at in the Scriptures, and have subsequently been developed in great deal by theologians and philosophers, often with considerable input from Greek philosophy. Many lists of divine attributes have been drawn up over the centuries, but I'm not going to quote any one of these in particular. Different Christians believe different things about God's qualities, and my list below isn't exhaustive. I've tried to stick with qualities that most Christians agree upon, but there are bound to be Christians out there who will disagree with some of these. All this is unsurprising, given that one of the things we definitely agree upon is that God is greater than human minds can comprehend.

Some of the things Christians believe about God are self-explanatory, but I'll go into a bit more detail for a couple of the more oblique qualities.

- God is love. We're told this specifically in the first letter of John in the New Testament, but God's love is attested throughout the Bible, both Old and New Testaments. Christians believe that God's love was shown in its highest form in God's coming to us in the human form of Jesus, living, teaching, healing and finally offering himself up to suffering and death.
- God is unknowable. This comes up throughout the Bible.
- God is just. He is concerned with justice, in how people treat one another, especially the vulnerable and helpless. God's justice is prevalent throughout the Bible, but most particularly in the writings of the Old Testament prophets.
- God is holy. This means he is absolutely free from sin and incorruptible.
- God is infinite. This refers to God's eternity, meaning that there is no time when God didn't exist. The Bible speaks of God as timeless and everlasting. It also refers to God's immensity, meaning that God is so great he cannot be contained.
- God is constant. He's not capricious or fickle.
- God is sovereign. He does as he chooses.
- God is all-powerful, all-knowing, self-sufficient, he doesn't have a body, and is simple – meaning what he is, he is entirely.

- God is without gender. If he doesn't have a body
and isn't human, he can't have a gender. This is
agreed upon by most Christians in principle, but in
my experience is a concept that is rarely followed
through. The following are examples of where the
principle clashes with Christian practice.
  - We usually (but not always) use male pronouns
  for God. This is a hold-over from centuries of
  patriarchy. If human societies were used to
  power being held by the male, and God was
  all-powerful, it only made sense for God to be
  referred to as a male. That said, there are key
  points in the Bible when God is likened to a
  mother, and the Holy Spirit is often referred
  to with female pronouns. Neither of these
  quite right the balance, but at least indicate
  that using male language to talk about God is
  more about habit than truth. I could wish for
  Christians to pray to God with female pronouns
  and metaphors every once in a while, but many
  Christians find it intolerably jarring after a
  lifetime of using exclusively male language. I'd still
  like to see more of it. The only way it will stop
  being shocking and strange is if we get used to
  doing it.
  - Jesus was male. This is a fact. But the
  significance of this fact has been the focus of
  a great deal of debate, especially recently as
  women have pushed against the ancient pattern
  of power held almost exclusively by men, and
  in the Church, as women have campaigned to
  be allowed to practice ordained ministry. Does
  Jesus' maleness mean the second Person of the
  Trinity, the Son, is actually gendered? I would say
  not, but I'm sure there are Christians who would
  argue otherwise.
  - Jesus encouraged his followers to pray to God as
  'Father'. Does this indicate that the first Person

of the Trinity is gendered? Again, I would say
not, but centuries of praying to God as male has
cemented that idea in the Christian imagination.

The quality of God that has been hotly debated in recent
decades is the traditional idea of God being changeless and
thus incapable of suffering. This not only clashes with the
image of God in the Bible as responding to the world and its
people and changing his mind, but also excludes the helpful
idea of God experiencing suffering alongside his creation. For
myself, I think God can experience suffering and respond to
things happening in the world. I think both those things are
included in God's love, which for me is his primary attribute.

How do you think God impacts the world?

I think God is intimately involved in the world. I believe that he
loves the world and everyone and everything in it, and wants
the best for us. At the same time, I believe he wants us to
grow to maturity, and that involves making our own choices
and our own mistakes as a species. This means two things.
First, that God doesn't 'control' the world. I don't think that he
makes natural disasters happen or directly causes people to do
things, bad or good. Instead, he gives us 'free will' to make our
own choices and take our own actions. But, second, when we
look to him and ask for his help, he will respond to us.

Judaism and Christianity have thought of God as a parent
for millennia for good reason. A good parent doesn't control
every aspect of their children's lives, because they know those
children will never truly grow up if they aren't allowed to make
their own way. But a good parent will equally never abandon
their child and will always be there to help if they're needed. I
believe that both these things are true of God.

As for the question of how God responds when we ask for
help, I don't think anything is impossible for God. I believe that
in creation he created the universe, including all its physical
laws, so if anyone can break them he can. All the same,
although he can, I don't think God intervenes in that kind of

crude physical way very often. In my experience, help and answer to prayer usually comes in the form of personal help: being given extra strength, comfort or skill to face whatever challenge has given rise to my call for assistance.

Of course, the biggest way (apart from creation) that God impacts the world is through Jesus Christ.

Jesus Christ

What's so special about Jesus?

There are three things that make Jesus special to Christians. Well, there are loads, but they can usefully be divided into three categories.

First, Jesus is special because of who he was. Christians hold that it is because Jesus was both human and divine at the same time that he was able to change the world in the most fundamental of ways. We say that Christ was fully human and fully God, with those two natures permeating each other in the same way that we try to speak of the Persons of the Trinity permeating each other. In Jesus, God was tempted, suffered pain and humiliation, and died. And in Jesus, humanity overcame all those things and rose again from the dead.

Second, Jesus is special because of what he did. He taught. He healed. He suffered. He died. He rose from the dead. Some Christians will emphasise one of those actions over the others. It was popular for a while to speak of Jesus almost exclusively as a moral teacher, for example. And various denominations, especially from the Protestant traditions and the lower end of Church of England church tradition, will focus on Jesus' suffering and death on the cross as the most important things. But the fact is that all of those things are important. Individually they are impressive, certainly. Even people who don't believe in the existence of God will find themselves admiring Jesus because of the things he taught and the way he lived. But Christians believe that together all those things make Jesus Christ the most special thing ever to happen to the human race.

Third, Jesus is special because of what he does now.
Jesus isn't dead. He rose from the dead. And then he went to
where God is. Christians believe that he is alive and with God,
that he hears and answers prayers, and inspires, strengthens
and heals those who ask for his help. Christians, especially
from lower church traditions, will often talk about having a
personal relationship with Jesus, as he makes himself known
to us through prayer. On the other side of the spectrum of
church tradition, Christians from higher church traditions
will often talk about Jesus making himself known to us in the
sacraments, especially in his real presence at the Eucharist as
we break bread and share wine.

Do you believe that Jesus' mother was a virgin?

Some Christians definitely believe that. After all, God can do
anything, so causing a miraculous birth wouldn't be a problem
for him. For myself, though, I don't have strong feelings or
beliefs regarding whether or not Mary was a virgin. I find the
early Church's fascination with virginity, especially female
virginity, to be rather irrelevant and unhelpful. The idea of Mary
being a virgin shows up in two of the four Gospels (Matthew
and Luke), and seems to spring from a prophecy from the Old
Testament prophet Isaiah in which the prophet wrote that 'the
virgin shall conceive and bear a son'. However, the Hebrew
word that was rendered into Greek and translated as 'virgin'
actually means simply 'young woman'. With this reading of the
prophecy, Jesus could just as well be the prophesied Messiah
without any kind of supernatural birth story.

Then you've got the fact that God can do anything.
Surely Jesus could be equally fully human and divine if he was
conceived and born in a 'normal' way but chosen by God.
Frankly, I'm more concerned with the outcome – that Jesus
was who he was and was born – than with the mechanics of
how that happened.

Please note that I doubt that this is the majority Christian
view. Certainly in the early Church, Mary's virginity was
massively important to their theology. For me, though, Mary's

virginity or lack of it doesn't really have a bearing on my beliefs
about who Jesus was and what he achieved.

What makes you believe Jesus rose from the dead?

Simply, because Christianity exists. What makes you think he
didn't?

*Isn't it much more likely that Jesus didn't die on the cross – that he
passed out and they took him down by accident?*

I don't think so. Roman soldiers were pretty good at their
jobs. Failure to ensure that a condemned prisoner was duly
executed would have put their own lives on the line. Plus the
stories of the crucifixion in the Gospels speak about Jesus
being stabbed with a spear and 'blood and water' coming out.
For the blood to separate in this way would indicate Jesus had
been dead for a while.

   Even if it turned out that the legionaries were
incompetent and the spear to Jesus' side didn't happen,
it's hard to see how the half-dead Jesus who would have
awakened in the tomb would have been any kind of inspiration
to his followers. Why would the apostles go to their deaths
fearlessly proclaiming Christ's rising from the dead if they *knew*
he had escaped death by accident and was still on the run
somewhere?

*Or Jesus could have died and the disciples hallucinated his after-
death appearances?*

Grief does strange things, it's true, and often people will catch
glimpses of their deceased loved one in familiar surroundings.
However, in the case of Jesus, the sightings of the risen Jesus
were shared among many different people, in one case at
least, hundreds of people. Nor were these appearances of
Jesus isolated and fleeting. When he appeared to the disciples
he would speak with them, on several occasions he ate with

them, and they were able to see and touch the wounds he received on the cross. According to Acts, these appearances happened many times over the course of 40 days. All of this adds up to much more than a grief-stricken hallucination.

The disciples could have known Jesus had really died, but made up a story that he had risen from the dead.

I can't help but think that with all the persecution that the fledgling Christian community suffered in the next few years, one of them at least would have cracked and admitted the truth. But that didn't happen. Followers of Christ went to torture and death for saying that Christ had risen from the dead. There were no benefits for them in insisting Jesus had risen again. All it got for them was more suffering. Would they really do that if they knew for a fact that he was actually buried somewhere? I don't think so.

Perhaps Jesus just died, but the stories around him grew and grew until by the time the Gospels were written, things had been exaggerated to the point where people were saying he had risen from the dead.

The Gospels were definitely written a few years after the events of Jesus' life, but not that long after them. Most scholars date the earliest of the Gospels to within 40 years of Jesus' death and resurrection. Forty years isn't a terribly long time for the details of the historical events to have faded into myth, and chances are the Gospel-writers, if not members of the intimate circle of the twelve original disciples, were close to them and members of the communities they built. Plus, early followers of Christ were suffering and dying for their proclamations about Jesus' resurrection well before the Gospels were written. The very earliest form of Christianity wasn't spread by the written word, but by communities telling the story of Christ and the effect he had had on their lives.

What do you mean by 'Christianity exists'?

I mean that something caused those first disciples to be so certain that Jesus had risen from the dead that they were prepared to change their lives for ever, to risk imprisonment, torture and death and challenge the authorities under which they had lived all their lives. Something changed them. I believe that something was the solid conviction that Jesus had risen.

If the physical resurrection of Jesus proved to be false, would that affect your belief in Jesus as the Son of God?

Probably. If there was incontrovertible evidence that Jesus didn't rise from the dead that would prompt some deep reflection and soul-searching for me. It would mean rethinking a lot about how I understand Jesus to be the Son of God.

That said, my understanding of Jesus has never been purely intellectual. I have a relationship with him in the here and now, through prayer and spiritual experience. It is real, and stands on its own. The effect of such evidence on my current understanding of Jesus' life would be a drive to reflect theologically on how that experience could be and what it means.

Why is Jesus' death so important to Christians?

For all Christians, Jesus' death and resurrection mark the healing of the fractured relationship between God and humanity, and herald the beginning of a new era for the human race. Christians refer to this as Jesus having 'saved' us. However, how we think Jesus' death and resurrection achieve this varies widely from Christian to Christian and denomination to denomination.

'Saves' us from what?

Again, this will vary depending on which Christian you talk to. My answer would be that he saves us from ourselves.

Even if we don't believe in the literal truth of the Adam and Eve story (I don't), we do believe that it reflects a truth about the human condition. This truth is the fact that humans find it very hard to stay on the path of goodness, and veer off into darkness and evil at the drop of a hat. In theological terms, we understand this as humans veering away from God, whom we believe is the source of all life and light and goodness. To turn towards evil is to turn away from God. Moreover, when people find themselves in darkness and evil, they will very often find themselves stuck there, and seemingly powerless to stop hurting themselves and others.

While some Christians are happy to talk about evil without any kind of personification, some Christians characterise this turning towards and becoming trapped in evil as the work of the devil, whether he be understood as a personal actor, as a shadowy force of darkness, or even the sheer absence of good. I'll speak more about the devil in a minute.

So how do you think someone dying horribly is going to change any of that?

Well, first, it's not just Jesus' death that makes the change. It's his death and resurrection combined. How Christians think these two things change the world takes many different shapes and forms. I'll boil down the numerous different appearances of the belief that Christians call the 'atonement' into three basic shapes.

First, we have the idea that Christ's rising from the dead meant he defeated death and evil. His actions meant that death wouldn't be the end for people any more, and evil would no longer be the trap that it had been. So if we believe in Christ, we will be empowered to break free of the grip of evil and sin.

Second, we have the idea that Christ's suffering, death and rising again meant he took the punishment that should have been humanity's, for falling away from God's plan for us.

God punished Christ in our place, and now we don't have to pay the price for our own sin and evil.

Third, we have the idea that Christ's life, death and rising again provided an example to humanity, showing us the extent of God's love. If we believe in Christ, the power of this example means that we will no longer be tempted into and trapped by sin.

In practice, mine and others' ideas of what Jesus achieved are usually a mixture of all three of these, and theologians' thoughts on the atonement, while often focusing on one of these broad categories, will vary considerably. All of them, however, are about the mending of the broken relationship between God and humanity, and restoring us to where God originally wanted us to be: no longer trapped by our own evil and free to grow into his children.

Would aliens existing cause problems for the idea of Jesus saving the world?

I don't think so. God revealed himself to the human race in Jesus, but that doesn't mean that God might not reveal himself to theoretical alien races in their form as well. Might not all races have an incarnation of their own? This is all speculation of course, and different theologians might give you different answers!

Sin

What is 'sin'?

Sin can consist of both words and actions, and involves a turning away from God. Christians believe God has shown us what he wants from us, through Christ's new interpretation of the Jewish Law and the example and directions he gave us. Sin is when we do, or even think, the opposite, and usually takes the form of some kind of selfishness.

*So how do you think that could trap us? Surely we can choose
whether to do good or evil?*

Yes, we can usually, but how many perfect people do you
know? By ourselves we can't make the right decision every
time. Martin Luther had an interesting idea of sin as being a
twisting away from truth and goodness. The more we do it,
the more we become twisted in on ourselves until eventually
we're so twisted we can't even see where we should be.
That's what being trapped in sin is about. Christians believe
Jesus releases us from that trap if we believe in and follow
him.

*But being a Christian doesn't mean you don't do bad things any
longer. Look at all the awful things done by the Church, priests
and Christians through the centuries!*

This is true. Being forgiven and freed by God isn't proof against
turning away and doing bad things again. Again, Luther uses
the helpful image of Christians being like previously terribly
ill people recuperating. Moving from sick to well doesn't
happen overnight – it's a long and difficult process, often with
relapses. Christians believe we need God's forgiveness and
help all the time, and even then we will go wrong from time to
time. What shows us to be true followers of Christ is that we
recognise when we have slipped and get back on to the right
path. The difference from people who don't follow Christ is
that Christians are given the example and the practical help to
make that move back on to the path.

In general, though, goodness knows, Christians aren't
perfect, and that includes priests.

Are babies born with sin?

I firmly believe that they are not. The idea that babies are born with sin comes from the work of the theologian Augustine in the fourth century. He theorised that if the first sin was committed by Adam and Eve, and the tendency to sin was passed on to future generations, it must have a means of being communicated. The obvious way, he thought, would be through the act of sex. Sex was thus understood as communicating sin from one generation to the next. This was what has been known ever after as 'Original Sin'. The next logical step was to say that if the tendency to sin was passed on through sex, babies must have it before birth.

The Roman Catholic Church taught that if babies were to die before being baptised, and thus washed clean of this Original Sin, they wouldn't go to hell, because they hadn't actually done anything wrong, but they would go to an in-between place called Limbo and not to heaven.

The Church of England doesn't subscribe to this belief. However, we generally believe that humans have a natural weakness to turning away from God which we can't keep in check by ourselves. On its own it's not sin, and it's not communicated by anything in particular. The act of sex is irrelevant, since we're not talking about something that needs to be communicated as Augustine thought. This weakness is thus present in babies, but we can't call that tendency on its own real sin.

We believe that unbaptized babies will go to heaven, certainly not anywhere else.

Life after death

What do you think happens after we die?

I can't tell you exactly what will happen. I'm not sure. Neither church tradition nor the Bible give us clear and detailed instructions as to what happens at the moment of death. Even when it comes to what lies beyond death in general we have only very vague ideas.

There are some firm promises that I can hang my belief upon, though. First, in Luke's Gospel we have the promise from Jesus to the thief crucified beside him that 'today you will be with me in paradise'. After death there will be a time of being together with God somewhere else. Second, we have the message that Jesus' resurrection wasn't just for him, but would be extended to Christians and to the whole of the created order when the work of bringing it to its full completion was achieved. So, I believe that at some point in the future, who knows how far in the future, the universe will be remade and those who have died will come to life again.

What that life will look like, I don't know. Paul, in his first letter to the Corinthians, writes in detail about his hope in resurrection for everyone, but acknowledges that we don't know what it'll be like. All that is certain is that it will be crucially different from this life. There will be no suffering, no pain and no more death.

Do you believe in a soul?

I believe something of us continues even when our body has died. I don't believe in a soul that exists before we are born, though – that's an idea that has no basis at all in Jesus' teachings.

Do you think pets will go where we go?

Yes. That probably sounds really odd, doesn't it? But I do. If God will remake the whole of creation, I think that will include all life and not just humans.

Where does heaven come into all this?

Jesus doesn't ever talk about people going to heaven when they die. He mentions Paradise in Luke's Gospel, and talks

about being with the Father, but 'heaven' is a word we attach
to the concept of the place where God dwells, complete with
fluffy clouds and angels with harps. Since Christians believe
that God is measureless, infinite and present everywhere, I
don't really have an idea of a physical place where God lives.
My idea of Paradise is more about a spiritual closeness to God.
In any case, I believe that the end point of life isn't incorporeal
living with God, but new life in a new physical creation.

What about 'purgatory'? Do Anglicans believe in that?

Some do, mainly among those of a High Church tradition.
But the 39 Articles specifically rule out the idea of a place
of temporary punishment where sinners suffer for the sins
they've committed. I think most Anglicans would follow the 39
Articles on this one.

*Do you think someone's soul or spirit can hang around after
they've died?*

When I'm talking to bereaved families, either to prepare for
the lost one's funeral or just as general pastoral care, I often
hear the idea voiced that they think the person who has died is
still around. They talk about being comforted by the person's
presence, or being watched over.

   I can't say I've experienced it myself, and it's not
something we hear mentioned in the Bible. I think it's a
comforting idea, but it's not something I believe. All the same,
I'm sure love continues after death, and that even when
they're with God in Paradise, before the general resurrection
and the recreation of the universe, our loved ones will continue
to love and care about us.

What about reincarnation?

No, in general Christians don't believe in reincarnation. I
certainly don't. The Bible speaks about one new existence,

after the remaking of the whole created order, not numerous lives within the same un-recreated universe.

Do you believe in hell?

Not as in the classical picture of lakes of fire and demons wielding red-hot pokers. We have Dante's *The Divine Comedy* and Milton's *Paradise Lost* to thank for those ideas about hell, not Jesus.

I don't believe in some form of physical punishment after death. The loving God I see in Jesus Christ isn't someone I can believe would devise the concept of eternal torture, even for people who have done the worst things.

What I do believe in is separation from God. I believe that after death, we will meet God face to face. And at that meeting we will get to decide once and for all if we want to be his people. If we want to be with God, we will be changed as a result, and be freed from our sin. However, we have the choice to say no. If we do, the result will be separation from him, and thus no more life.

The Devil

Do you believe in the Devil?

Not in the one we see in medieval pictures: horned, forked-tailed, cloven-hooved and bright red. The entire story of angels falling from heaven, led by Lucifer, isn't Biblical at all. It actually comes from 1 and 2 Enoch, non-canonical books written around the second century BCE and used by a particular Jewish sect. The use of 'Lucifer' as the name of the leading fallen angel who became Satan actually comes from Isaiah chapter 14, and refers not to an angel falling from heaven, but to a Babylonian monarch. The stories around Satan have thus been developed quite apart from what we find in the Bible.

That said, I do think there is a weight in the universe that draws us towards darkness unless we push against it, whether that darkness be selfishness, sadism or despair. That force is sometimes personified in the Bible, as Satan in books such as Job, while sometimes it takes other names and forms. Paul in his letters, as well as mentioning Satan, refers to the 'rulers' of the world, whose control is broken by Jesus. He's not talking about earthly rulers like emperors, but supernatural forces.

Some Christians believe very firmly in the concept of an evil tempter who wants to draw all humanity into his clutches. I don't share that belief, at least, not in the idea of it being a personal force. I think it's larger, more formless and less personal than that.

Why not a personal devil?

I can't square the idea of a totally good God who has created a good universe creating a being capable of being or becoming the incarnation of evil. For me, the concept of a good creation means that however wrong people may go as they use their free will, they are capable of being redeemed. There is always some good in them. I can't see where the good in Satan would be.

What about demons?

No, I don't believe in demons. Again, there are Christians who do, and the concept of demonic possession is still held in some quarters. Personally I think the idea of demonic possession in the Bible is more likely to refer to mental illness than actual possession by demonic forces, making Jesus' healings of demoniacs physical and spiritual acts of healing. For me, if the devil isn't a personal force, he doesn't need other personal beings to do his bidding.

Angels

What is your belief about angels? Actual beings that reside in the heavens? Or fiction?

Angels are a bit more complicated for me. Messengers from God show up a lot in the Bible. Sometimes they look just like normal people, which is often the case in the older portions of the Old Testament. An obvious example is when three angels visit Abraham, who sit and eat with him and look perfectly ordinary. Whereas sometimes they are terrifying beings, bright and shining and powerful, whose mere presence makes people collapse in front of them from fear. This is the case in the book of Daniel, where the writer sees a vision of a terrifying angelic figure. In the same way, the angel mentioned in Luke's story of an angel coming to Mary to tell her she would give birth to Jesus is a fearful figure. In both cases the angel has to tell the person being visited to 'not be afraid'. The simple name 'angel' is by far the most commonly used name for God's messengers.

But just to make matters more confusing, the Bible also refers to beings thought of as serving God in heaven, named cherubim and seraphim. Cherubim is the name used most often, and it is these winged beings that are carved on the top of the Ark of the Covenant and that stand guard over the Garden of Eden. Cherubim are usually named in the context of their place on the Ark, but the one major exception to this is the book of Ezekiel, where Ezekiel has a lengthy vision involving cherubim in chapter ten, where they are operating some kind of mysterious wheeled structure.

Seraphim are named only twice in the Bible, both in the book of the prophet Isaiah, where he has a vision of being in front of God in the Temple. They are described as having six wings: two to cover their faces, two to cover their feet, and two with which to fly. Apart from the wings and the fact they have faces, feet and hands, Isaiah tells us nothing more about their appearance.

The sheer weight of references to these servants and messengers of God in the Bible (nearly 300 references, direct and indirect) makes me think that God indeed has messengers that he uses to communicate with the world. We know very little about them, and I'm open to the idea that in some cases God uses ordinary people to speak through, but as far as I can see, there isn't a good reason to reject the idea of God creating other spiritual beings who serve him in this way.

The end of the world

Have you given much thought to the apocalypse? Will it be an act of God?

I've given it some thought, certainly! One of the key elements of Christian belief is that we believe the world will come to an end at some point. Since the life and development of the world is and has always been in God's hands, we believe the end will also be his own act. What form it will take, and when it will happen, is impossible to say.

I don't think that it will be exactly the process described in John of Patmos' vision in Revelation. This is because John is writing in a genre called 'apocalyptic', which isn't so much about predicting the future as it is protesting the present. Scholars generally accept that by means of coded language (how many horns a beast has, for example), John's vision is attacking particular political figures of his day and encouraging his fellow Christ-followers to stand firm despite the persecution they're suffering.

What Christians do believe for certain is that Christ will come again before the end, making himself obvious from the very beginning this time. He will come in glory, and remake the whole of Creation, including resurrecting those who have died.

Loads of Christians seem to make a hobby out of predicting the end of the world. Do Anglicans do that?

Thankfully not as a rule. Jesus is quite clear in the Gospels that no one knows when the end will come. He says that there will be signs of the impending end, like earthquakes, wars and famines, but these will be only the very beginning of the process. The end will come when the sun is darkened and the stars fall from heaven, and then Jesus himself will return. Most importantly for this question, though, he says in Mark's Gospel: 'But about that day or hour no one knows, neither the angels in heaven, nor the Son, but only the Father' (Mark 13:32). With this kind of flat statement from Jesus himself it's amazing to me that any Christian would then try to calculate dates and predict when the end might be as if the Bible was some kind of giant code. It isn't, and any kind of prediction will be a misleading, manipulative waste of time.

Could the apocalypse be a result of something humans do, like a nuclear war that destroys the Earth?

I don't think so. It's entirely possible that the human race might destroy itself at some point in the future, given the stockpiles of nuclear, chemical and biological material that the nations have created. But there is nothing to say that our wiping ourselves out would trigger the end of the universe as a whole. I think God's plan is bigger than that. The absolute end will be something God does, not something we do to ourselves.

Non-believers

What does it mean for religious belief that there can be perfectly virtuous people who don't believe in God?

I don't think believers have a monopoly on virtue – I'd have to be an idiot to suggest it. The thing is, we are none of us perfect, believers or not. It is my belief that following Jesus, trusting in God's love and forgiveness and acceptance, makes it so much easier to live a virtuous life. Some people have amazing inner strength, and can lead lives of astonishing virtue without explicit reference to God. But even they are not perfect, and most of us can't hope to have that kind of strength of will. Knowing that I am loved and accepted even when I fail is a great source of strength for me: a strength that I couldn't hope to produce on my own.

What do you think about people who are members of different religions?

I believe that there is one God, and that everyone who seeks to know their Creator and to do his will is moving towards the same God. Mark's Gospel records Jesus saying to his disciples, 'Whoever is not against us is for us' (Mark 9:40). Anyone who holds Jesus in esteem and is trying to do God's will is working towards the same purpose.

Now, I'm a Christian priest. It won't be a surprise for me to say that I think Christianity is the best route to knowing and following God. I believe that Jesus Christ is the ultimate revelation of who God is, and that walking his path and trusting in him is the surest way to live the life God wants of us. But I don't think that other faiths are automatically wrong. In fact, I'm certain that all faiths that are trying to know God have something valuable to share, and that Christians would do well to listen to those outside our faith. We all have a lot to learn about God, after all.

Do they go to heaven? Or is Gandhi in hell?

As I already mentioned above, the only hell I believe in is separation from God and true end of life. I believe God values all goodness, and that as long as a person wants to be with him then they will be welcome.

What happens to all of those people who lived and died before Jesus was even born? Do they get to go to heaven and be with God?

I believe they do. You see, I understand Christ's life and death and resurrection as events that aren't limited by the passage of time. Christ makes right peoples' relationships with God in the past as much as in the present or future. So, deep in the past people will never have heard the name of Jesus, but his life and acts fundamentally change the nature of creation, them included. And much as I believe God values goodness in people since the time of Christ, I believe that he values goodness whenever it occurs in the history of the world.

Sacraments

What is a sacrament?

In the catechism (a set of questions and answers about Christian beliefs originally designed to be learned by heart) included in *The Book of Common Prayer,* a sacrament is defined as an 'outward and visible sign of an inward and spiritual grace'. In other words, a human ritual or action using particular physical elements is not only understood as a symbol of a divine action, but is also understood as a sign that involves that divine action being brought into effect. So even as physical actions are taking place, inward changes are also occurring, thanks to God's power.

So you tell God to do something and he jumps to it?

No. Christians don't believe that by doing particular things they make God do something else, as if certain words and actions constituted some kind of magic lever. God's actions are always freely given (hence 'grace'). But we understand that God has promised us that he will act in certain ways if we call on him. Sacraments are about obeying the instructions God has given us, not the other way round.

As I mentioned earlier in the section on the modern Church of England, different groupings of Christians believe that different rites can be considered to be sacraments. Everyone agrees on the two sacraments that are instituted indisputably by Jesus in the Gospels: baptism and the Eucharist. The other various rites (seven for the Roman

Catholics, two or three for Lutherans, innumerable for Greek Orthodox Christians) are more debatable, and the Church of England itself manages to hold within itself Christians who cover the whole range between the Roman Catholic doctrine of seven sacraments and the Reformed doctrine of two.

Do you believe the bread and wine actually turn into Jesus' flesh and blood during a Holy Communion service?

I don't, no. Some Anglican Christians, usually from the high end of church tradition, believe that they do though.

When do they change? Do you taste blood in your mouth?

Anglican Christians who believe that the bread and wine literally become Christ's body and blood (a belief called 'transubstantiation') hold that the change occurs during the Eucharistic Prayer, during the words of institution: 'This is my body … do this in remembrance of me.' This is also the Roman Catholic teaching. Orthodox Christians, on the other hand, believe that the change is a longer process, beginning with the Liturgy of the Preparation, which is the private preparation of the bread and wine before the public part of the service, and ending with the 'epiclesis', the invocation of the Holy Spirit upon the bread and wine.

Crucially, those consuming the consecrated bread and wine won't notice any physical difference about them. Inside and out they will taste the same, look the same and, to all appearances, be exactly the same. Believers in transubstantiation, following the concept of appearance versus substance that was first expressed in Aristotle's *Metaphysics*, hold that the outer appearance of the bread and wine remain the same while their inner substance changes. They *are* the body and blood of Christ, while retaining the physical appearance, smell, taste and feel of bread and wine.

But you don't believe they change? What does Holy Communion mean to you then?

Christians who don't believe the bread and wine literally change into flesh and blood still believe that something mysterious and important is happening during Holy Communion. Luther taught that Christ could be really present in the bread and wine without needing them to literally change. Zwingli, on the other hand, argued that Holy Communion was purely symbolic and memorial in character (hence Jesus' 'do this in remembrance of me'), and Christians didn't need to bend over backwards trying to work out how Christ could really be there in the bread and wine while they remained looking and tasting like bread and wine. Zwingli still taught that Christ was really present at Holy Communion, only Christ's presence was among the congregation, not in the consumables.

For me, as for many Christians, Holy Communion symbolises and involves a number of things. It brings believers together in unity as they share in the bread and wine. It both recalls Jesus' words and actions at the Last Supper and symbolises the time when all believers will be together with Jesus in the new creation, sharing a new and different meal together. As we celebrate together I believe that Christ is indeed truly present, both among the congregation and in the bread and wine.

Holy Communion is celebration and thanksgiving and statement of intent all at once and there is nothing else like it.

Why do people sometimes just open their mouths for the vicar to put the bread into?

On one level this is a hold-over from medieval times, when priests would only put the bread into people's mouths to make sure they actually ate it. This was to prevent people taking the bread away with them rather than eating it, and doing superstitious things like burying it in the corners of their fields because they thought it would protect their crops. On another level, refusing to touch the bread is a sign of respect and awe for the presence of Christ within it.

What do you believe is happening at baptisms?

Just like Holy Communion, there are a number of things going on in a baptism service, and some of the symbols have more than one meaning. Being submerged in (or sprinkled with) the water of baptism represents two things: being washed clean of sin, and dying to the old sinful life and rising again to new life, just as Christ died and rose again. In baptism Christians believe that we are being forgiven our sins and welcomed into and empowered to serve among the people of God, which is to say, the Church. Various other symbols are also used in services of baptism: anointing with the cross, showing that we are claimed by Christ and reminding us of his death for us on the cross; and the giving of a lighted candle, symbolising Jesus the light of the world, and the fact that the baptised are to live in the light of Christ.

I've heard it said that it's a good sign when babies cry at baptisms. Why is that?

It's an ancient folk belief about baptism. The idea is that as baptism washes away sin, it also drives out the devil. When a baby cries, they say, that's the sign of the devil leaving them. Superstitious folk even thought that it was a bad thing for a child not to make a fuss, and babies who were too contented would find themselves being pinched to make them cry.

Thankfully it's not something I've ever come across as being seriously believed any more.

Ethics: What Christians believe they should (or shouldn't) do

Homosexuality

Do you think homosexuality is wrong?

I don't. I'm not alone in this thought both among other clergy and Anglican Christians in general, but equally there are plenty in both those groups of the opposite opinion.

I don't think it's wrong because I firmly believe that being gay (or for that matter, being wherever you are on the broad spectrum of possible sexualities) is something you are born and not something that you choose. It isn't a 'lifestyle choice': it's a fact of being. On the understanding that all sexual activity is practised only between consenting adults, there is no harm to be done and a great deal of good for people to live freely and openly as what they were born to be.

Why would Christians think being gay is a bad thing?

Two things. First, there are a number of passages in the Bible that can be taken to mean that God regards homosexuality as a sin. These add up to eleven passages in total, five of which are indisputably talking about homosexuality in general and not about rape or cult prostitution in particular. Three of these are in the New Testament, and one of them includes lesbianism as well as gay male sexuality. In the context of the Bible as a whole, this isn't much screen time, but the argument is that these are five instances of homosexuality being condemned, which is five more than there are of homosexuality being endorsed.

Second, Christians tend to appeal to the Natural Law ethical system, which defines as good that which is fulfilling its God-given natural purpose. Under this system of thought, human sexuality's 'good' end is procreation. Therefore, any kind of sexual activity that definitely won't result in babies isn't 'good' activity.

There's a possible third reason, which is less of an argument and more of a visceral feeling. There is still a kind of gut-level discomfort among many people with the concept of homosexuality, and this combined with the above arguments can make a heady mix.

But you don't agree?

No. The arguments from the Bible don't add up to an unassailable case for me. First, and most importantly, the Gospels, and Jesus in particular, have nothing to say about homosexuality. As far as I'm concerned this indicates that at the very least, homosexuality was desperately low on Jesus' list of priorities of things to change about the world. At the most, it may indicate that Jesus was actively welcoming towards gay people in the same way he was welcoming to the other 'outcast' groups of his day.

Second, I think it's pretty clear that these prescriptions against homosexuality are more about the culture of their time than about unchangeable commandments from God. After all, we've discarded the vast majority of Jewish Law as listed in Leviticus, including commandments not to have sex with a woman in the week after she's had her period and to never blend two fabrics in the same garment. Why, then, do we feel we have to hold on to this one law in particular? The pronouncements in the New Testament are similarly culturally flavoured. The passages that clearly refer to homosexuality in general come in Romans, 1 Corinthians and 1 Timothy. Much of the Church is happy to dispense with other pronouncements from the New Testament letters, such as that slavery is an acceptable state of affairs and that women should either never speak at worship or that they should only speak if they have their heads covered. Again, I don't see why we should hold on to the words against gay people in particular.

Finally, in the past the Church shamefully used explicit statements in the Bible to defend the practices of both slavery and apartheid. We recognised in those cases that although we might be proposing the letter of the law, we had lost the spirit of Jesus' message of love and acceptance for all. I believe it's the same in this modern furore about homosexuality.

As for the Natural Law argument, the fact is that in nature there is the same bewilderingly large spectrum of sexualities that we see in the human race. Dolphins, for example, will engage in same-sex sexual and courting behaviours. Female Laysan Albatrosses will pair bond with other females to co-operatively rear their young, engaging in courtship behaviours and nest-building together. Basically, creatures of the same sex engaging in sexual behaviours together is perfectly 'natural'. This rather sinks the argument in the water. Similarly, this lingering visceral discomfort with homosexuality that some people experience is more about what were previously accepted as cultural norms than about some kind of moral insight.

Is there something about same-sex marriage in particular that raises people's blood pressure? Recently it seems as if Christians are more exercised about the idea of gay marriage than about gayness in general.

Well, yes. We've already looked at the arguments Christians sometimes advance against accepting homosexuality. When it comes to the question of marriage we have the added complication that the Christian Church, and Jesus himself, have always defined marriage as being between a man and a woman. To allow same-sex marriages is thus a major redefinition.

So why would you want that redefinition to go ahead?

First, I think it's appropriate to recognise the close bonds of love that bring together same-sex partnerships as much as heterosexual partnerships. On the assumption that God creates people with their different sexualities, I believe it's right for Christians to accept that those sexualities are good. Thus when they find expression in a loving, committed and lifelong relationship it's appropriate for us to recognise and invoke God's blessing upon that union.

Second, marriages aren't all about procreation. In the reasons given for marriage in the Church of England's *Common Worship* marriage service Preface, procreation comes second to the 'delight and tenderness of sexual union and joyful commitment'. Many marriages either cannot result in children, due to the age or fertility of the couple, or will not, thanks to the free choice of the couple not to have children. We still accept those marriages as full and right. Why change the rules when it comes to same-sex partnerships?

What do you think about same-sex marriage?

I think it's a good thing and it will be a tremendous step forward if and when the Church finds itself able to conduct such services.

Will the Church of England conduct same-sex marriages in the future?

I really hope so. In reality, though, I don't see it happening for a long time. Considering the many decades it's taken us to get as far as we have with accepting women's ministry in the Church, and the fact that feelings run so high on this issue, I think it's going to take a while. That said, I hope and trust we'll get there in the end.

What's the situation with gay clergy?

The Church published its guidelines on issues of sexuality among its clergy back in December 1991 under the title *Issues in Human Sexuality*, and hasn't revised its position since. All

those going forward for ordination have to have read these
guidelines, and have to agree to practise their conclusions.
One of these was the statement that homosexual people were
allowed to be ordained so long as they were celibate.

This is still the case today. Things got a little more
complicated in 2003 when there were protests raised over the
prospect of an openly gay man being ordained bishop. This
caused the issue to be debated again by the House of Bishops,
with the conclusion that again, as long as the person was
celibate, being homosexual should be no barrier to becoming
a bishop. It has yet to happen in the Church of England, but I
think it will be a matter of only a short while before we have
our first openly gay bishop.

As we saw earlier, other Churches in the Anglican
Communion don't hold the same opinion. In The Episcopal
Church in the USA, gay and lesbian Christians have become
bishops already. Conversely, there are conservative Anglican
Churches, especially on the African continent, that are
expressly against homosexuality in general and homosexual
clergy in particular. The fallout from this clash of opinions
threatens to split the Anglican Communion down the middle.

Sex

Do Christians think sex is bad?

I'd like to say no, but I think in practice that plenty of Christians
do think that. It's a frame of mind that's hung on from St Paul's
encouragement for people to stay celibate if at all possible
because it was better for their spiritual focus and relationship
with Christ; and from Augustine's teaching that the act of
sex was what passed on Original Sin from generation to
generation.

Although neither of those things are still taught or
believed in the Church of England, the general attitude
persists.

I much prefer the attitude that you find in the Old
Testament, which recognises sex as a wonderful gift given

by God, to be enjoyed and celebrated, within the context of God's blessing and the institution of marriage.

What do you think about sex before marriage?

Sex has a great deal of emotional, physical and spiritual power, and as a result we need to treat it with respect. I firmly believe that people should only have sex within a loving, committed relationship – ideally one which is either already bound by marriage, or at the least which shortly will be bound in that way. Where we go wrong is when we engage in sex without thinking about the consequences, and end up losing self-respect or respect for others. If we treat our bodies purely as objects we lose something very important.

The worst situations are where people are pressured into having sex that they don't really want. Going into sex reluctantly, just to please someone else or because someone feels it's necessary to become properly 'adult', is a recipe for disappointment and low self-esteem.

But surely hardly anyone waits to be married before having sex these days?

This is true. Of all the marriages I've conducted so far in my ministry, every single couple were already living together before deciding to get married, many of them for years.

But just because something rarely happens in practice or is hard to achieve doesn't mean it isn't something worth aiming for.

Why bother to get married?

From a Christian standpoint there are two main reasons. First, it calls a couple to commit themselves to each other, before all their friends and family and before God. In response to this commitment, we ask God's blessing upon their union, which is one of the most joyful things I get to do as a priest. There's nothing like pointing people towards the realisation that the

God who is love blesses their love. Second, it provides a unity and a stability that is really important, especially in cases where the couple wish to raise children. But even if they don't, marriage is far more than just a piece of paper. It changes people from two separate individuals into a united team: it changes how they see themselves and how others see them, both in a very positive way.

War

Can Christians fight in wars?

There are plenty of different views on this. In the history of the Church it became an issue the moment soldiers began to want to follow Christ, and became an issue of crucial importance when the Roman Empire adopted Christianity as its state religion.

The fact is, if we were just sticking to what Jesus had to say, we would be strict pacifists. 'Turn the other cheek' and 'pray for those who persecute you' are pretty clear instructions. Nowhere does Jesus encourage his followers to take up arms against those who would do harm to them or others. There are plenty of Christian pacifists out there today, and some denominations are expressly pacifists, such as the Quakers.

What about if you're attacked?

Well, yes. Human beings are belligerent. They fight at all levels of society and especially when it seems that talking isn't going to get anyone anywhere. Worse, there are situations when a person or a group or a nation is going to do their best to hurt or kill others whether or not the other side wants to fight. Unprovoked attacks are common. So what do Christians do when they, or their loved ones, or their group, or their nation, is attacked without provocation. What do you do when turning the other cheek just means that you end up on the wrong end of a sword/gun/invading army?

Some Christians hold fast to the pacifist ideal, and say that we should accept death as a possible consequence of bearing witness to Christ in the world. It's the price that must be paid, and even if it doesn't change the world in the immediate short term, it serves the Kingdom of God in the long term.

Others say that we can't serve God if we're dead, and advocate fighting back, so long as the violence is limited and justified. This is the idea developed by Augustine in the fourth century, and is known as the 'Just War Theory'. Augustine suggested war was moral and permissible as long as it satisfied a number of criteria: it should only be declared by a legitimate authority; it should only be fought for a just cause (such as defence of others as opposed to personal greed or ambition); it must be a last resort after all other options are exhausted; it must be defensive; force used must be proportional and the safety of non-combatants must be assured; it must have definite goals and have a reasonable chance of being won; it must not be waged looking for unconditional surrender, and it must not be prolonged.

What about if you've not been attacked yet, but you know it will almost certainly happen and that if you let the other side prepare the war will be that much worse?

This is the next level. These days with sophisticated intelligence at our disposal, developed nations can reasonably predict when they are likely to be attacked, by whom and with what. What then is the morality of a pre-emptive strike?

Again, there are Christians who would say either that any violence is prohibited, or that we must wait until we are actually attacked before violence is justified. However, there are Christians who would argue that in the interests of saving more lives, a preventative war is acceptable.

What about you?

I'm with the second of those options: that fighting back when attacked is permissible. If I or my nation were to be attacked, and the ensuing violence would respect the limitations suggested by Augustine, I think it could be justified. But it would really have to be the absolute last resort.

Evangelism

What do you consider to be the nature and extent of your obligation to evangelise?

'Evangelism' is an interesting term in that it means different things to different people. For some Christians it is a positive word, meaning both speaking and living the power of the good news of Christ. But for some Christians the word is tied to a negative image of tiresome people standing on street corners and browbeating people into taking leaflets. That kind of aggressive evangelism has never held any attraction for me. It seems to be more likely to drive people away than to encourage them to follow Christ.

Where most Christians agree is in the use of the term 'mission', which covers the positives of the concept of evangelism without the negatives. It stems from the idea that God is a God of mission, meaning that he is constantly reaching out to others in love. In response, his Church should be doing the same, not just to get more people coming to church on a Sunday (although that's always nice), but to change the world for the better. Mission might include activities like community volunteer work, raising the profile of social justice issues, visiting the sick or prisoners and so on. The idea is that we do all these things as Christians, not hiding who we are, and being ready to talk about our faith if asked, but equally not pushing what we believe into others' faces. Actions speak louder than words, after all.

With this definition of mission, I'm not sure there's a limit to its extent. Ideally, wherever I am, whatever I'm doing, I'm doing it as a representative of Christ and am ready to talk about what I believe and how it shapes my life whenever someone asks.

What do you think of retro missionary work – people from former colony nations coming to Europe to perform missionary work?

It's rather embarrassing, to be honest. It's embarrassing that it's necessary. Although it's no longer the case, there was a point in the twentieth century when the Church of England was definitely in decline. There's a whole generation out there who know hardly anything about Christianity, because when they were children their parents saw no reason to take them to church or Sunday school. So there is a genuine need now for people to learn about Christianity for the first time. The Christians who set about reaching out to those people have to be fiercely passionate about their faith, and many of them do indeed hail from places where believers from the Church of England were the ones doing missionary work over a century or so ago.

I suppose the right term is 'humbling'. It leaves us in no doubt that Christ and Christ's work aren't about us – they're about him. If we fall behind in doing his work, there are others out there who will step up. It's an object lesson that arrogance has no place in Christ's Church. I hope we learn it well!

The environment

What is the Christian viewpoint on the changing environment? If God is all-powerful, can't he just put it right?

If we're just talking about God's power, then yes, of course he could put everything right. But we're not. Christians believe that God created the entire universe, with living creatures being the crown of that creation. Humans in particular, created and called to be God's people, are given free will to grow to maturity as children of God, not his puppets. One of the truths that I believe lies at the heart of the Genesis creation stories is that the human race has been given special responsibility over the world. We aren't just put here to dominate the world around us, we are to be its stewards. That means we don't just do what we want with the world – we are chosen to oversee and care for it.

With this in mind, humanity's abuse of the world, the deforestation, the extinction of so many different species, the global warming, the growing acidity of the sea … all of this is laid at our door. God isn't responsible for it – we are.

There's a school of Christian thought that says God is going to end the world and re-create it at some stage in any case, so why worry about the state of the environment now? They're missing the point. God created the world and gave it into our care. If we believe in God, and in the truth at the heart of the Genesis stories, there is no justification we could make which would excuse us from trying to do our best for the world.

Politics

What do you think a vicar's role should be in political/social change, if any?

I think vicars have to be involved in political and social issues. It always makes me laugh when the Archbishop of Canterbury, for example, writes an opinion piece or speaks to television news and criticises some aspect of policy, and immediately there's a slew of people coming forward to criticise him for being so 'outspoken'. It's as if some people out there believe a vicar should be seen and not heard.

Well, I'm afraid that's not how it works. Jesus, whose example we follow, was hugely outspoken to those in power. He criticised those who didn't take care of the poor, those who looked after themselves before others, those who built up their own wealth at the cost of those around them. Were he incarnate today, I have no doubt at all that he would be doing exactly the same thing. Archbishop Rowan Williams, speaking as he often did about social justice and care of the poor and dispossessed, was frequently accused of being 'left wing', 'liberal' or 'socialist' as if they were bad things. Jesus would be speaking about exactly the same issues.

Yes of course Jesus also spent much of his time speaking about the Kingdom of God, the newly re-created world ruled by God alone that is to come, but that isn't to say that all social and political change should wait for that day. Jesus also taught that Christians' social and political beliefs and actions should anticipate that rule of God. We are called to act as if the Kingdom has already come, not to put off those right actions for when it's already here.

However, that's not to say that I think vicars should be involved in party politics. They should definitely speak to politics as the framework that governs how people live, but things become problematic when the Church allies itself with one particular party against another. Our role is a prophetic one.

Prophetic? You want to predict the future?

Thankfully not. I mean prophetic as in the Old Testament prophets. They weren't interested in predicting the future, but instead were about criticising structures and behaviours and provoking change in the present. Like them, we need to be the people who aren't afraid to point out when things are going wrong, even if that creates powerful enemies for ourselves. We need to be on the outskirts, speaking up for the people who have no voices.

Again, it's an ideal, but one I hope we strive to live up to.

Should the pulpit be used to discuss things of a political nature?

Not regularly, I don't think. Services of worship aren't synonymous with political rallies, and there are other times and places when those discussions can take place. Every so often, though, I think it's important to engage with political issues. Christianity isn't a faith that can be neatly separated off from the rest of our daily lives. If we do it right, our faith shapes and drives every other aspect of who we are. If our belief in Christ didn't ever impact upon our political thinking, we would definitely be doing it wrong.

Farewells

With that, we've come to the end of this question and answer session. Well done for making it through to the end! I hope you've enjoyed it, perhaps learned something, perhaps had a few new questions and discussions prompted for you. An FAQ like this can't answer all the questions you might ever have, but if it's primed you to go out and ask and debate more, I think my work here would be done.

Where do you go if you want to know more? Your first stop is your actual vicar. You know now that the Church of England is an established Church, so even if you've never actually met him or her, you have a vicar there for you. Buttonhole them! Not every vicar will be able to field your questions off the top of their heads, but I think they'll be glad to be approached, and hopefully able to point you towards answers even if they can't provide them themselves.

If what you're after is further reading, there's a lot out there. Here are a few of my major sources, favourites and recommendations:

On ordination and vocation: John Pritchard, *The Life and Work of a Priest*.

On spirituality: Gerard W. Hughes, *God of Surprises*.

On prayer: Joyce Huggett, *Listening to God*.

On church history: Diarmaid MacCulloch, *A History of Christianity*.

On Christian beliefs: Colin Gunton (ed.), *The Cambridge Companion to Christian Doctrine;* Blackwell Companion volumes, especially the *Blackwell Companion to Modern Theology*.

Thanks and Acknowledgements

A few words of thanks before I go. I could never have written this book without the steadfast support of my wonderful husband Paul Cornell, who was called upon for everything from question phrasing to childcare. Thanks also to my super editor David Moloney, whose advice has made this book much better than it would otherwise have been.

Beta readers and expert advice from: Jim Barlow, Tim Barnard, Tim Harper , David Robinson, Christopher Woods, Helena Thomas, Claire Hayes, Rupert Bursell.

Grateful thanks are due for all their feedback. All errors, of course, remain my own.

Questioners on social media: sorcha, Peter Anghelides, Francesca, David Weller, Julie Farmer, Teresa Jusino, Carol Robinson, Steven Stone, Alan MacKenzie, Chris Lewis, Steve Margolis, Vicky Symcox, Gary Riddle, Marja Flipse, Mary Fleeson, Jonathan Rose, ickle tayto, Martin Curnow, Russell Hillman, Joe Black, John Toon, Siskoid, Johnny Nexus, Kat Keen, Sally, Paul Gadzikowski, Adele, Guy Robinson, Martha Hubbard.

Index